How I trust Shelley Hendrix! She is winsome and delightful while deeply thoughtful and filled with grace. This is not a book of technique but a way of living. She writes with conviction, vulnerability, humility, and authenticity. Shelley has fought hard for these truths. She will not try to teach you what she is not committed to living through. Her words are from God's own heart and are vitally transformational.

John Lynch, coauthor of *The Cure, Bo's Café,* and *On My Worst Day*

Whether you've been hurt by a family member, work for a difficult boss, or are having problems with your best friend, this book will equip you to navigate relationships in a God-honoring way, bring peace to your life, and help you become a more loving person.

Pete Wilson, pastor and author of *Plan B*

Girls...you will love this book! In a world that pressures us on every side until it's hard to catch our breath, Shelley shows us how to breathe deeply and lean into God and His Word. She reminds us that God is always in control and nothing is wasted in His hands. Breathe, girls...breathe!

Sheila Walsh, Bible teacher and author of *God Loves Broken People*

Why Can't We Just Get Along is a wonderful extension of Shelley Hendrix's ministry to women. Every woman will see herself in this book and discover God's grace to help them face the challenges of relationship.

Ken Davis, Christian comedian and author of *Fully Alive*

This book is a resource for women who have been wounded by relationships yet still yearn for real friendship and authentic community. With powerful, profound insights from Scripture, this is a book you will want to read more than once and pass on to your friends too. Shelley doesn't just bandage the wound and promise it will get better—she shows readers *how* healing will happen and *Who* they can trust. This is a must-have, must-read book!

Ginger Garrett, author of *Beauty Secrets of the Bible, A Woman's Path to Inner Beauty,* and *Chosen: The Diaries of Queen Esther*

D1045373

Shelley Hendrix approaches the often overlooked subject of interpersonal relationships with a beautiful balance of boldness and grace. Filled with stories of firsthand experience in the delicate dance of female dynamics, Shelley helps readers overcome past hurt and fear to live in the freedom of God-led friendship. This is a must-read for every woman.

Jessica Wolstenholm, blogger and author of *The Baby Companion: A Faith-Filled Guide for Your Journey to Motherhood*

Reading this book is like meeting a friend at a cozy tea spot, crying your eyes out about someone who is treating you badly, and then receiving encouragement and strategies for finding your way. Every reader will resonate with how awful it feels to wonder, "Does this person dislike me? Is she being mean on purpose? What should I do now?" Shelley gives plenty of tangible help—not just spiritual platitudes—and God's Word is woven into every page.

Lucille Zimmerman, Licensed Professional Counselor and author of *Renewed: Finding Your Inner Happy in an Overwhelmed World*

Shelley Hendrix lives her life with a fragrance of grace. She captures this essence in her stories and life examples. Rarely is a book both delightful to read and relevant to our daily struggles. Shelley offers her relational life experiences with the practical application of godly principles. Reading this made me want to give one to every one of my friends!

Brenda Wagner, PhD, clinical psychologist

Why Can't
We Just
Get
Along?

Why Can't We Just Get Along?

SHELLEY HENDRIX

HARVEST HOUSE PUBLISHERS
EUGENE, OREGON

Cover by Dugan Design Group, Bloomington, Minnesota

Cover illustrations© iStockphoto / cinnamonsaturday, P2007

Back cover author photo by Amelia Grace Photography

This book contains stories in which the author has changed people's names and some details of their situations in order to protect their privacy.

WHY CAN'T WE JUST GET ALONG?
Copyright © 2013 by Shelley Hendrix
Published by Harvest House Publishers
Eugene, Oregon 97402
www.harvesthousepublishers.com

Library of Congress Cataloging-in-Publication Data

Hendrix, Shelley, 1974-
    Why can't we just get along? / Shelley Hendrix.
        p. cm.
    ISBN 978-0-7369-4864-7 (pbk.)
    ISBN 978-0-7369-4865-4 (eBook)
    1. Christian women--Religious life--Textbooks. 2. Female friendship--Religious aspects--Christianity--Textbooks. 3. Female friendship--Biblical teaching--Textbooks. I. Title.
    BV4527.H463 2013
    248.8'43--dc23

                                                            2012026071

Printed in the United States of America

13 14 15 16 17 18 19 20 21 / BP-JH / 10 9 8 7 6 5 4 3 2 1

To the woman who has helped to shape me most

Beth Turner

You are my mom and a safe confidante in a world where trusting others can be a challenge. Thank you for cheering me on these past few years and for believing in me and the call of God on my life. I will always be in your corner. And I will always make sure to bring chocolate.

xoxo

Acknowledgments

It is so hard to narrow my expressed gratitude down at all. So many people have made investments in my life that have made this project possible. But I would really be remiss not to acknowledge these individuals and groups here:

To my best friend, Stephen Hendrix, who swept me off my feet and gave me his name: Thank you from the bottom of my heart for being you and giving me the safest place on earth to be me. There is no way I'd be in ministry at all, much less in a position to have anything to put on paper for others to read, if not for your incredible support and encouragement. *I still can't believe I get to be married to Stephen Hendrix!*

To my children, Amelia, Macey, and Jackson: Thank you for your patience with your mom while she was typing away at all hours of the day and night to get this book written. You probably made the biggest sacrifice of anyone so that this idea could become a reality and I want you to know that I recognize this and appreciate it so much. I love having a front row seat in your lives!

To my parents, Lewis and Beth Turner: Thank you for being the first ones to teach me about the One who loves me most and for pointing me in His direction from before I was even born. So much of what I've learned, I've learned from you both. So much of who I am is because of you. I love you and I am so thankful you're my parents.

To the women of Church 4 Chicks: I would be remiss not to thank you all for believing in this ministry's purpose and mission and for going the extra mile. I especially want to say thank you to Debra Courtney who has walked this journey with me from the time God put the vision in my heart and mind. You are a woman of incredible integrity, loyalty, tenacity, and courage. No one celebrated this book with me more than you, Deb. I will always be so grateful!

To my amazing and wonderful publishing team at Harvest House: Bob Hawkins Jr., thank you from the bottom of my heart for believing in the message and for seeing value in me. Your leadership is inspiring as you humbly, yet boldly, lead your team to publish books that we can believe in. LaRae Weikert, thank you for a forever friendship that allows us to work on projects we both believe in so much. Kathleen Kerr, I could not have requested a more fun or more fabulous editor for this project. Your enthusiasm and support have meant the world to me. All along the way, you have been the voice of a cheerleader! To the entire HH Family: You all welcomed me into the circle as though I'd always been here. You've given your best and you have honored Christ. I am amazed that I get to work with you all. "May you be richly rewarded by the Lord for what you have done…"

To Rob and Ashley Eagar of Wildfire Marketing: WOW! You took this message that was good and using your insight, input, and tell-it-like-it-is approach turned it into something great! I am elated to work with you both and thank God for allowing me the privilege of working alongside of you to make this message even clearer and more effective. May your tribe increase as you help communicators share their message!

And to some of the biggest heroes in my life:

Ginger Garrett: Thank you for teaching me that sometimes God allows one of His kids to get ahead of the other so that she'll be in a good position to open a door.

Babbie Mason: Thank you for believing in me and in the ministry God has called me to lead. Your life, ministry, and example have meant the world to untold thousands upon thousands and yet you took the time to influence and invest in me individually. I am overwhelmed by this reality and by our friendship.

John Lynch, Bruce McNicol, and Bill Thrall: Without the influence of TrueFaced Resources, I doubt this book or this ministry would even exist in the way that it does today. As God was revealing truth to me about His grace and wooing my new nature to come out to play, it was your voice more than any other that helped me to trust His. I owe you a debt of gratitude that I will never be in a position to repay. Thank you, thank you, thank you—for not only being voices of truth to this chick's life, but also for being my friends. I am so honored to be a part of your tribe.

Sheila Walsh: Thank you for taking the time to encourage other women all over the world—including me. Your life, example, friendship, and support mean more than I have the power to express here. I am so thankful for you!

Contents

Foreword

By Babbie Mason

It deeply blesses and greatly impresses me when I meet young Christian women who have a passion for God's Word and the ability to articulate that passion to communicate His message to the lost, the hurting, and the next generation. Shelley Hendrix is one of those young, passionate, articulate women who, out of the overflow of her relationship with the Lord Jesus, is pursuing God's call on her life to teach, lead, and encourage other women. *Why Can't We Just Get Along?* contains a powerful, insightful, and relevant message for the age in which we now live. As we navigate home life, work, play, and worship, the opportunity is great that we will encounter difficult people, even people we know, are related to, and claim to love; even people who profess to know Christ. Out of her own experience, even her own pain, Shelley Hendrix digs deep to remind us that often the roadblocks to relationships begin and end not with the other person, but with us. Shelley reminds us that God's Word is the quintessential relationship manual. And whenever and wherever people encounter one another, there is that great possibility that disagreements will arise. In her powerful and poignant manner, Shelley helps us discover that the most powerful ingredient to any and every relationship is the power of God's love. And through that love—the deep, sweet, love of Christ, we can get past tolerating each other to bask in the joy of celebrating each other.

Shelley's masterful teaching helps us to examine our own hearts and lives to begin enjoying the rich and satisfying life Jesus intended for us to live—together. Whether reading Shelley's books or hearing her as she teaches and mentors women across the street or across the country, she is on a mission, fulfilling the Great Commission and making a difference. God is using Shelley Hendrix, and He will use this message to change your heart and life. I know—because it's changed mine.

Babbie Mason
Award-winning singer, songwriter, and author

Introduction

"Why can't we all just get along?!"

We've all asked this question and most of us have asked it more often than we can even remember. It is frustrating enough to be disrespected by some random stranger in traffic, and something completely different to be shown disrespect by a person who is a part of our everyday lives—someone who should know better, someone who should be too mature to treat others the way they do.

The book you hold in your hands speaks to the topic of relationships—those we hold near and dear as well as those we would like to see *disappear*. It's so important to get this right. If we can be successful in our relationships, we can be successful in life. The reverse also holds true. If we don't learn how to be successful in relationships, we will not be successful in the other areas of our lives. Our relationships carry extreme significance!

How to use this book

Because we retain what we participate in far more than we retain what we only hear or read or see, the book you hold in your hands has been designed so that you (and hopefully a few others along with you) can take part in a journey as you reflect upon what you've read, respond to the questions posed, and act upon the practical principles shared throughout the pages ahead. The questions are, for the most part, open-ended, encouraging you to spend more time in honest communication with yourself, your heavenly Father, and perhaps with a trusted friend or group of friends. Don't worry too much over whether or not you answered the questions correctly. If you are answering honestly, then you are answering correctly.

Additionally, you will find a guide in the back of the book which is there to help you with some conversation starters as you take your journey one step further (again, hopefully with others). If you happen to read this book solo, please consider going through and completing the questions in this section of the book as well for your own added benefit. (But do consider asking someone to join you in this journey—the extras you get as a result are totally worth the effort!)

In the following pages, we will take steps together on the path to finding peace. I've included true stories—including several of my own—that help to illustrate the very real-life stuff we'll talk about and face together. Other stories come from the lives of women from all over the world and from the pages of Scripture as well. Additionally, we'll take pause from time to time to give ourselves some encouragement from the Word of God, others' lives, and how God works in and through our everyday *stuff* as we learn to trust Him more and more.

Like the sign that hangs on the front door of my gym says, "The first step is showing up." Let's get started, shall we?

Relationship Quiz

Check all that apply to determine if you are in a *Why Can't We All Just Get Along?* relationship:

☐ I face family functions with trepidation based on who I'll have to spend time with while there.

☐ I have a love/hate relationship with women at church. I love to go to church, but I hate the pressure I feel to measure up to certain women.

☐ I no longer attend church because of the experiences I had with women there.

☐ I love Jesus. It's His children I'm not too fond of.

☐ I tend to keep most women at arm's length because I've seen that women can be untrustworthy.

☐ I share little of my life, emotions, and opinions with most women because it just isn't worth it.

☐ I have a lot of acquaintances but almost no real friends.

☐ It is difficult for me to be around people who are not like me.

☐ It is challenging for me to be around people who have opposing beliefs.

☐ I am so tired of feeling pressure when I'm around other women.

☐ I feel judged and criticized by other women.

☐ I feel pressured to be someone I'm not with certain people.

☐ I often "get back" at other women in my mind rather than confronting them in person.

☐ If I had known that my marriage would include his family, I might have run the other way.

☐ I think my children/parents/in-laws/step-family plot against me when I'm not around.

☐ It is very difficult for me to trust other women.

☐ I would like to have closer relationships with women, but I honestly don't think it's possible.

☐ Can't we just keep pretending everything is okay?

I have good news. If you checked any or even *all* of the above, you are going to get a *lot* out of the pages to follow!

Part One

Let's Be Honest: Relationships Are Tough!

Here we are: at the starting line. But this isn't a race to see which one of us is a faster runner and this isn't about getting ahead of one another. This is more like a journey that must be taken together—step by step. If at any point you get stuck, discouraged, or afraid, I want to encourage you to invite someone into your struggle. Let someone know what is going on with you (preferably someone who is taking this same journey with you), and let that person's strength and courage carry you for a little while. You never know, she just might need you around the next bend.

1

It's Not You. It's Me.

The two women exchanged the kind of glance
women use when no knife is handy.
ELLERY QUEEN

I could not believe it!

I could not even believe she did what she did. It didn't seem to matter what I did or how hard I tried to be friendly and supportive, she insisted on insulting me every chance she got. And it wasn't like we were kids or even teenagers—we were both grown women! It seemed that every time we were in the same place at the same time she found ways to insult and injure me. I tried to give her the benefit of the doubt each time: *Maybe she doesn't mean anything by this. Maybe I'm just being too sensitive. Maybe it's that time of the month...*

But this...This took the cake! We had already known each other in our tight girlfriend group for years. And because we have mutual relationships with others, we all happened to be at the same place at the same time for a dinner together. Again. I could tell when I was also invited to this meal that it made her uncomfortable—even unhappy.

As we all sat together sharing conversation, I thought I tasted something in the main dish she had brought. Something serious. Something

I cannot eat. Something that everyone knew from a previous episode that I absolutely could not eat!

I decided that as much as she might not like me, she would not go so far as to put something in the food that she knew would make me sick. Would she? I convinced myself that I was mistaken and that no adult would do something like that to another adult. And certainly not a Christian adult. Right? While I was mulling those thoughts over in my mind, one of the other ladies who was sitting with us looked at her and said, "This isn't a secret ingredient. It's…"

I realized suddenly that she had purposely added the unnecessary ingredient. The one she knew I couldn't eat. She hadn't warned me about it. But apparently she had told at least one other person at the dinner that she had added a "secret ingredient" and decided it was information not worth passing along to Yours Truly. To top it off, it seemed that she even thought this was funny! I've never asked people to make special concessions for me based on what I'm able to eat and not eat, and had she mentioned it I would have gladly chosen to enjoy the other side dishes. I was caught completely off guard. I didn't know what to do or how to respond. Stunned, I thought to myself, *Is this really happening?*

It seemed like a weird alternate reality had taken over. The clock stood still as I tried to make sense of a senseless situation. It felt like everyone was watching me, waiting to see how I would react.

In my passive insecurity, wanting everyone to like me and not wanting to rock the boat, I said nothing. Nothing! But on the inside, I was about to explode. I stopped eating the dish she'd prepared and discreetly covered what was left with my napkin. I excused myself to go to the restroom so that I could have a few minutes alone to deal with what I knew was a really unpleasant expression. I prayed. Hard. And then I returned to the table. Again, I said nothing. Later that night, I was sick and miserable. But more than that, I was so hurt and confused…and yes, very angry!

For me, this was the final confirmation that for whatever reason this woman just did not like me. But it was worse than that. It was more like she wanted to make sure I knew she didn't like me and that I was not welcome in her life. She was always competing, always putting me in my place. Not liking me I could deal with. It was her unrelenting antagonism that was getting to me, especially since we were around each other so much.

I stayed up through the night dealing with very uncomfortable physical symptoms (I'll spare you the details) and crying out to God. As my mind played the same mental motion picture over and over again, rehashing all the times she had insulted me, my children, my opinions, and my choices, I didn't know who to turn to. No one could handle my anger and confusion—no one except my heavenly Father. I was at a loss. This relationship had gone from cool, to cold, to downright ugly. And I had no idea why. A hundred thoughts ran through my mind:

We don't have to be best friends outside of this group, but why can't she just be nicer at these gatherings? Why does she have to even be here? Should I just have it out with her in a knock-down-drag-out right here and now? Or is there a better way to handle this than wishful thinking or complete avoidance? What should I do about this? What awful thing have I done to deserve this kind of mistreatment? Why does she insist on hurting me so intentionally and at every opportunity? Am I so unlikeable that someone would be so antagonistic so often? Maybe it's me? Is there something wrong with me?

Why?

It has been said that our greatest wounds come through our relationships. I don't know about you, but in my experience the biggest challenges I have faced haven't been financial, physical, or circumstantial—although I've experienced all of these. What has kept me awake at night and has most occupied my thoughts during the day are messy relationships. More than any other challenges, broken relationships and dealing with difficult people (or even dealing with great people in difficult circumstances) have the power to throw my world out of whack.

Some of these people have been authority figures, some coworkers, some relatives. Some have been people I could avoid for the most part, and others were those I couldn't avoid at all. Some of these wounds came through words said; some came through words left unspoken that I longed to hear. Some wounds came through physical acts against me and some were the result of nothing more than a simple misunderstanding.

It was one thing to deal with this issue in childhood. Kids are still figuring out how to work and play with each other, and we expect a certain amount of immaturity in their relationships. I was one of those girls who always got along better with boys...and I knew why. Girls were mean. But aren't adults supposed to know better? Weren't we supposed to figure out how to play nice back in preschool?

And here's the real kicker: The majority of my most challenging relationships were with those inside the church. I wish it weren't true, but my most pain-inducing, heartbreaking, gut-wrenching relationship struggles have been with others who claim the Name of Christ just as I do. After a while it just got to be too much for me to be around those individuals or groups when weighed down by the pressure I felt in their presence. Pressure to measure up, pressure to walk on eggshells because I didn't know how they'd react to what I might say, pressure to please so that I could avoid their criticism or condescending remarks. As a grown woman and, more importantly, as a child of God, I knew He wanted something better for His girls.

Through these experiences, I got to a point where, in my exasperation, I finally threw my hands in the air and cried, "Why can't we all just get along?" I was tired of trying so hard to make peace with others who seemed to have zero interest in pursuing peace with me, and I was sick of the pressure I felt around my sisters in Christ. I tried a lot of different tactics to make peace. For a while, I even tried to pretend I didn't care.

It didn't work.

Eventually, in my desperation, and as I cried out for the umpteenth time to my heavenly Father, I began to hear His voice leading me and guiding me to His path of peace—peace that is not on offer in the magazines at the grocery store checkout line or on any of the social network sites. I was desperate for help and my heavenly Father was gracious to offer it. As I asked the Lord over and over what I should do about all the broken relationships I was seeing, God used the words of the apostle Paul found in Romans 12 to radically and forever change my approach to handling difficult relationships—and the people who don't seem to care whether or not we get along with one another. I was desperate for help, desperate for answers, and you know what? I found what I was looking for!

As I bawled my eyes out to God, Romans 12:18 came to mind: "If it is possible, as far as it depends on you, live at peace with everyone." This verse of Scripture played over and over in my mind like a song on repeat, and it sounded good. It sounded really good. And for about five minutes, I felt the weight on my shoulders lift a bit. I took in a deep, calming breath. *If it is possible... as far as it depends on me...* But then, as I played those words over in my mind once more, I began to wonder, *Lord, just what is up to me? What am I supposed to be doing? What haven't I tried? Isn't this supposed to be about the other person changing her ways?* As I opened God's Word to the surrounding portions of that same verse in Romans, I knew I was on to something that would change every-thing. Romans 12:18 reminded me that God's Word really does speak to every situation we face and that we can get the best strategy for suc-cessful living if we'll allow His Word to do its job in our lives.

In my dealings with the woman at the beginning of this chapter, I had been trying for years to either get her to like me—or, failing that, to put her in her place so she'd stop putting me down. I just wanted to end the drama between us and I wanted to know how to do it. As I began to apply to my own life what I learned in God's Word over those next few weeks and months, I was actually surprised to find that these principles were working. I was feeling greater peace and less pressure even though nothing in the relationship had changed...at least as far as the other woman was concerned. I then took what I was learning and tried it out on the women who attend Church 4 Chicks. I knew this stuff was good—even life-changing—but I had no idea how much it would impact women as they heard and then applied these principles.

It is now my privilege and delight to journey with you through the six principles I learned. I've never been a good salesperson. If you want me to sell something just to sell it, I'm not going to put much effort or passion behind it. But when I believe in something because I've tried it out myself and found it to be the real deal, it becomes natural for me to want to get others in on the good thing I've found. When I witness its power in the lives of others, my loyalty to it is only solidified! This is such a treasure. God's Word is powerful and alive and it is still changing lives after all these thousands of years. I'm full of hope and expectation as you read and apply what you learn and watch your relationships be transformed.

It is true that our greatest wounds come through relationships. But it is also true that our greatest healing comes from the same place. So maybe, when there doesn't seem to be a way forward, the answer *isn't* cutting off contact and removing yourself from a relationship (although at times that is a necessary option). Maybe God wants to do something even better!

What have you tried in the past to help you in these types of relationship struggles?

How successful have you been as you've tried these solutions?

When You Know Who You Are, You'll Know What to Do

Several years ago one of my favorite people passed away. Her name was Audrey, but no one called her that. She was just "Honey"—Aunt Honey to me, as she was my grandmother's sister.

Aunt Honey told the best stories. One of my favorites was the story of one of her brothers who, as a young man, served his country in World War II. He was wounded in battle and lost his dog tags—along with his memory. He didn't remember who he was and had no idea where he was from.

No one knew exactly what to do with him. He spent about a year recovering in an army hospital in Idaho without any clue as to his true identity. His family assumed he had died along with the rest of the platoon. Without dog tags, he was just another John Doe.

Can you imagine the uncertainty? The fear for the future? His inability to go forward? Can you imagine the effect on the family? The grief, trauma, and confusion that comes when a son and brother is declared missing-in-action?

Thankfully, another soldier from back home recognized my great-uncle and helped reunite him with his family. When my uncle didn't know who he was, he was lost. He didn't know what to do. He didn't have any direction in his life. Until someone else was able to reveal his name and his true identity, he was limited in what he could do, where he could go, and what decisions he could make. The best part of Aunt Honey's story was when she told of the reunion. After the long months of silence, he strolled up the street to his home and his family's warm embrace. He was lost no longer. He had a name, and he could begin to live out of that reality.

Before we get too far into this book, it's vital that we build our strategy for peace upon the most solid foundation. My hope is that this book will be like that soldier in the army hospital, revealing who you are according to what God says and thereby giving you the confidence to live out of who God says you are. When you know who you are, you'll know what to do. Conversely, when we don't know who we are we won't know how to respond when faced with both challenges and opportunities.

WWJD?

I was in my teens when the WWJD craze hit. Even people who didn't follow the Christian faith were wearing the WWJD bracelets. *What would Jesus do?* The question was everywhere. How would Jesus handle this situation? How would He respond? How would He act?

You see, everything Jesus did was based on who He *was*. Jesus was God's Son—the One in whom the Father delighted. But Jesus wasn't just God's Son—no, it gets even better than that! According to the Scriptures, Jesus was and is *God*. When we read stories about Jesus, we are reading about God Himself—and we discover that at His core, He is love (1 John 4:8). Love isn't merely an attribute of God's character. God *equals* love!

Everything Jesus did on Earth flowed out of that love. He performed miracles, told parables, confronted religious leaders, hung out with society's rejects, fed thousands, faced His own death, died, and rose again because of His love—because of *who He was!* Because He knew who He was, He knew what to do.

When we believe that we are responsible for living in a way that will please people, we will never be at peace. There will always be pressure— pressure to do more, be more, strive harder. When we don't measure up or reach that goal, we'll decide it just isn't worth it. We'll give up. Stop trying. Avoid the challenges that will make us grow. We're acting not out of love, but out of fear. Doesn't sound like something Jesus would do, does it?

How can you identify with the pressures to strive harder and the pressures to give up?

Not only do we need to know who we are in order to know what to do, but we also need to know what's already been done for us so that we don't spend our lives spinning our wheels, desperately trying to achieve something that has already been accomplished by Someone else. We'll get to that in a bit. Hang tight.

Out of Sight, Out of Mind?

The relationship I shared at the beginning of this chapter was one that I couldn't avoid completely. Truth is, I didn't want to avoid it—at least at first. I wanted to find peace, experience restoration, and even enjoy the times we were together. This was the relationship that I kept grieving over and struggling with—the one that kept me wondering, "Why can't we just get along?" Eventually, I gave up and quit the pursuit for peace with her. It was time for a break, and I knew I was driving my husband absolutely crazy as I wrestled with it over and over and over again with him as my sole audience. Since I knew I didn't need to gossip about this woman to others, I bounced my questions, ideas, and tears off of my wonderful husband, who, I'm thankful to say, survived the whole experience with me. (And in spite of me!)

For a while, giving up felt good. Pretending was less painful than acknowledging the hurt. But the peace didn't last very long.

We can't escape this completely.

We all have someone in our life who is hard to get along with. It could be someone you work with or attend church or school with. It could be that one family member who makes family get-togethers seem totally not worth attending…or at the very least, makes you fabricate an excuse to leave as soon as you can. It could be your boss or teacher or neighbor.

Why do some people just have to be so difficult to get along with?

Who comes to mind right now as you read this? Put her initials or some other identifiable, but discreet, indicator here:

Some of us will need to take an honest look in the mirror, because there is a good chance that although we can all name at least one difficult person in our lives, we've all *been* that person at some point along the way. Sure, we can blame the devil, or our hormones, or that other person, or unlikeable circumstances, but in the end we have to take responsibility for our part of the problem.

Ever heard the line *The devil made me do it?* It was an expression popularized by Flip Wilson in the 1970s. And, although Flip was being…well…flip about the whole "devil made me do it" thing, we can all relate to some degree. We've all made decisions that seem counterproductive and foolish. But when we know who we are, we know what to do. We know what our responsibility is and what isn't. We know that no one—not even the devil himself—can make us do anything we don't want to do. When we don't know who we are, we spend our time, energy, and resources trying to "fix" the people and circumstances in our lives. We shift blame, we manipulate, we pout, we make concessions. Knowing who we are frees us from this damaging cycle and frees us to be fulfilled and active participants in the Body of Christ.

Personal Response

In light of what you've read in this chapter, jot down some of your initial thoughts about your relationships and what God might be teaching you through them.

In your experience with difficult people, jot down some of the solutions you've tried and how effective they were.

As you read God's Word, what is the Holy Spirit revealing to you about difficult people in your life?

Dear heavenly Father, as we take our first steps on this journey towards finding peace in our relationships I ask that Your Holy Spirit be completely free to do His work in our hearts and lives. Give us the grace to take an honest look in our own mirrors so that we'll see ourselves and others more clearly. In Jesus's name, amen.

Check out more from Shelley at
www.shelleyhendrix.org/2012/07
/sometimes-you-hurt-my-feelings.html

2

What's Love Got to Do with It?

You have never lived an unloved moment in your life.
MAX LUCADO

I knew a pair of sisters who were only about a year apart in age. These girls fought like cats over everything: boys, clothes, cars, attention, friends...you name it! I would feel so uncomfortable around them when they would get into it—usually over a sweater that one wanted to wear when the other didn't want her to wear it. And when I say they got into it, I mean they got *into* it. They would claw at each other. Pull hair. Bite. Scream. It was ugly. And all of this because of a sweater?

We often allow such minor issues to become major obstacles to peace. If I don't know who I am, if my worth doesn't come from the knowledge that I am a beloved daughter of the Supreme Lord over all creation, then I'll let something like a sweater get the best of me too.

A woman named Julie told me, "I've had friends who have told me that they desire to have a 'real' relationship with me... a 'deep' friendship. But when it comes to opening up something is missing: trust. You can't have a real, deep relationship unless there is mutual trust. I believe people really want to be loved but they fear trusting one another with their deepest places." Can you relate to what Julie shares? What do you think is at the root of this fear of trust?

In 2011 I went on a mission trip to West Virginia. We were working in McDowell County, and I kept seeing landmarks pointing out sites of the Hatfield-McCoy feud, the biggest family feud in American history. During their long-lasting feud in the late 1800s, over a dozen family members were killed and their saga made the national headlines. And the *really* crazy part of it all is that the feud began because one family claimed ownership of a pig that the other family insisted belonged to them. A pig. You can't make this stuff up.

What comes to your mind when you think of families feuding with one another? Do you know of a current family feud? If so, how did it begin?

Family feuds are nothing new to the human story. Think about Cain, the first son of Adam and Eve, who killed his brother, Abel, out of jealousy over God's favor. Or think of two sisters, Leah and Rachel, who ended up married to the same man (talk about dysfunction!) and dealt with some major feuds over the years. (I am so glad I never had to go to *their* house for the holidays!) The list goes on and on, but one of the starkest examples is that of two sisters who got to sit in the very presence of the Son of God and still had trouble getting along with each other. Let's take a quick peek into their story together:

> As Jesus and his disciples were on their way, he came to
> a village where a woman named Martha opened her home
> to him. She had a sister called Mary, who sat at the Lord's

feet listening to what he said. But Martha was distracted by all the preparations that had to be made. She came to him and asked, "Lord, don't you care that my sister has left me to do the work by myself? Tell her to help me!"

"Martha, Martha," the Lord answered, "you are worried and upset about many things, but few things are needed—or indeed only one. Mary has chosen what is better, and it will not be taken away from her" (Luke 10:38-42).

Martha and Mary no doubt loved each other deeply, as we can see in other portions of the Gospels. It is also apparent that they both loved Jesus and that He loved them as well. But for most of my life I heard this passage taught in pretty much the same way: "Be like Mary, and don't be like Martha." I think the story is deeper than that, however. Let's take a closer look.

Notice in this passage that Martha had invited Jesus into her home and that she was simply doing what she knew how to do: She was being hospitable to her guests. She had found her affirmation as a woman in her gifts of service and in being able to make people feel welcome. Mary, on the other hand, was more at home at Jesus's feet. Mary's desire to be with Jesus mirrored His own longing to be close to His friends.

When Martha finally got fed up, sick of working so hard without the help or affirmation she craved while Mary did nothing and got plenty of Jesus's attention, she did not lash out at her sister or even go out and nudge her discreetly to come help. Who did Martha fuss at? She fussed at the very one she called *Lord*. She questioned whether *He* cared about her, whether *He* saw what she was doing, whether she was as important to Him as her sister was—you know, the sister who was just sitting there doing nothing! She said what we have all felt: "Lord, don't you even *care?*"

One of the most critical people I've ever encountered is a woman who is good at everything she attempts. But she's also exhausted most of the time. Looking back on my life, I believe I was headed in this same direction until God mercifully allowed me to experience extreme failure and loss. When we allow our abilities to determine our value, we are only setting ourselves up for heartache and loneliness. We are not the sum total of what we are able to achieve. Who we *are* is far more important than what we can do. Who we are is a constant. What we can do can change in the next breath.

It only takes a second for everything to change. And if we find our value and worth in what we are able to do, what happens when we can no longer perform? Models grow old and are replaced by younger talent. Athletes are injured and can no longer compete. Surgeons lose their dexterity and cannot operate. Will they despair, feeling that their lives have come to nothing? Or will they find their worth in a power greater than themselves?

We've all heard the saying *Hurt people hurt people.* This is truer than we might realize. Wounds are inflicted by those who ask a deep, unspoken question in their hearts: "Am I loved?" "Am I valuable to anyone?" "Does anyone *really* care?"

In this chapter, we'll look at the importance of genuine love. We will understand how we love others best when we realize how much we are already loved ourselves. I can only imagine the difference this understanding could have made for the sisters with the claw marks all over their arms after their fight over a sweater, or for the Hatfields and McCoys in their feud over a pig. If Cain had understood how much God loved him, would he have murdered his brother in a jealous rage? And if Martha had been as confident as her sister that she too was deeply loved by her Savior, might she have enjoyed sitting at His feet for a bit rather than feeling unseen and unloved?

It's strange to think that we don't live our lives based on who we are. We live our lives based on who we *believe* we are, and much of what we believe about ourselves is the result of what others have said, done, or neglected to say and do. In my own life, I have given others the power to determine my value and my worth. Why do we allow broken, imperfect people to define us by their opinions, actions, and words— or absence thereof? Our innate desire to find acceptance and avoid rejection can wreak havoc in our lives and how we view ourselves.

When you know who you are, you know what to do. How do you see this play out in the story of Mary and Martha?

As true as it is that hurt people do in turn hurt other people, it is also true that loved people love other people. Oftentimes, our struggles in relationships happen because one or more of the persons involved believe that they are not truly loved. They can't move past their insecurity. We are "acceptance magnets" because we were created to be loved. You are designed to hear someone say "I love you" and mean it with all their heart.

We have listened to the lies of the enemy for far too long, thinking that our difficult experiences confirm the untruth he speaks. *You're only worth what you can do,* whispers the enemy. *You deserve everything that's been done to you. You deserve to struggle today.*

I knew a woman who once told me that whenever she was in situations involving other females, she always felt like she was on the "wrong side of the door." All the other women clicked with one another, but she never did, and she wasn't really welcome to join them in their circle. She said she could picture all the women enjoying their time together in one room while she was always on the outside of the door—close to what was going on, but not invited in to be fully a part of it all.

Another woman shared with me that she didn't just feel left out or unworthy—she actually felt *toxic*. Due to unimaginable abuse endured during her childhood, she believed the lies that the enemy spoke through those experiences told her (Hey, if God really loved you as much as He loved others, why would He let this happen to you?). She lived for a long time in dysfunction, believing those lies were true. Did this trauma impact her ability to relate well to others? Of course it did!

For me, I knew "in my head" that God loved me, but my experiences and faulty thinking caused me to stumble in my belief that God really and truly loved *me*. Just as I am. And I know I'm not alone in this. I hear from far too many people in far too many places to believe this is my own unique struggle. We all deal with insecurity to some extent. When we realize we aren't alone in the fight, we open ourselves to opportunity. We can begin to relate to others on a deeper level—the same desire Julie shared at the beginning of this chapter.

My husband was once leading a discussion about the unconditional love of God. He asked people in the group if they "felt" God's love and trusted it. Everyone acknowledged their struggle to really believe—with their whole hearts—that God loved and *delighted* in them. Everyone, that is, except for one woman. She said, "I don't struggle with this. I know God loves me and I know He delights in me." To which my wise husband replied, "How do you know?" She began to share Scripture with him, but it didn't sound like it was really coming from her heart. My husband asked, "If you were lying in a hospital bed, and you were unable to do anything for God, all you could do all day would be to lay in that bed, would He delight in you then?" The woman quietly and slowly responded, "How could He?"

Why do you think we tend to base our value and our worth upon the external results of what we are able to do? How have you seen this hurt relationships?

What could be different about your current relationships if each party was able to embrace their identity based upon a relationship with Christ rather than on each person's abilities or lack thereof?

There is a saying that is fitting here: "The ground is level at the foot of the cross." How might it change the climate of your local church, family gatherings, small groups, etc., if each person began to adopt this reality?

We Are the Church

I believe that one of the main purposes of the Church—not the building we enter on Sundays or for special occasions and holidays, but the Body of Christ, believers—is to demonstrate genuine not-of-this-world love to others. God's love is poured into us, and as we experience its truth and power we can, in turn, let it flow outwardly to other members of the Body. Christ told His followers, "By this everyone will know that you are my disciples, if you love one another" (John 13:35).

We find it hard to recognize God's love for us if we have never felt a genuine human expression of love. God wants us to love one another well—and I don't just mean husbands and wives. I mean believers, family members in the household of faith. God's purposes for us are so much bigger than *just* us.

One of the ways Satan works to cause dysfunction in our relationships with one another is to get us to believe that God doesn't *really* love us—at least not as much as He loves other people. He'll point out all those comparisons that, when added up, create some pretty incriminating circumstantial evidence against a God who declares Himself to be very good, but doesn't always *appear* (at least to our eyes) to be so.

I heard one person share that our concept of God is built on a combination of our understanding of God's Word and the personal pain we've experienced. This is a power-packed thought, don't you think?

Do you agree with the above "formula"—that your concept of God is based on your understanding of His Word as well as the pain in your past? How have you experienced this in your own life?

How can we alter this "formula" to help us have a healthier, more accurate concept of God?

When we perceive that God loves another person more than us, or that other people have had a better hand dealt to them, we can feel threatened as we compare our lives with others'. This happens all the time—more than any of us probably realize or feel comfortable enough to admit. Comparison is like our shadow—we can't seem to get away from it! When we walk into a room, we immediately notice every other woman. We take a mental inventory—*Is she prettier than me? Thinner? Better dressed?* When we walk into someone's home—*Is her house nicer than mine? Bigger? Tidier? Better decorated?* We compare kids, pets, jobs, marital status, grades, job performance, social status, finances....everything!

Something inside us craves validation, and we seek it out without even realizing what we're doing. Comparison only breeds contempt and dissatisfaction with our own lives—and our own identities. If we know who we are—and whose we are—we'll be comfortable in our own skins instead of sensing that constant pull to compare and resent the people around us. (And how can you have a relationship with someone you resent?)

I worked with a support group of women, all ministry wives, for five years before launching Church 4 Chicks. One activity we did at different times and with different women was a drawing exercise where each of the ladies was asked to draw something pertaining to the topic we were walking through and dealing with together. Once we all drew pictures of God. Of course we do not really know what He looks like, but we all do have some kind of imagery in our minds when it comes to Him. Drawing this out on paper opened our eyes to what our hearts really believe about Him. In some cases it revealed what we were afraid was true, but never allowed our minds to fully express. For example, one woman drew an angry male figure wearing a black robe. He was sitting behind a judge's bench and getting ready to slam his gavel.

Sometimes what our minds think and what our hearts feel don't match up. It is important that we learn to be honest with ourselves and with God about what is true in both of these areas of our lives.

Think about it. When you hear another mom brag about her children's successes while yours go from one struggle to the next, something doesn't sit right. Or when that woman in Bible study gets to go on yet another exotic trip with her husband and family while you are struggling just to make ends meet, something doesn't sit just right. Or when someone complains about her extra five pounds of weight while you've been burdened by the twenty-five that will not budge, something doesn't sit right with you. When you've been trying so hard to do the right things and bad things keep happening, when someone who doesn't even seem to care about doing good finds success at every turn, something doesn't sit right. When one person's business or ministry seems to be thriving while yours is barely sustaining itself, something within us feels robbed. It feels like there is an imbalance in the universe. It is not *fair* that life does this to us.

And for those of us who believe there is a Creator who is in charge of it all, it can seem as though that Omnipotent Someone is holding out on us while blessing the fuzzy socks off of someone else.

If you struggle with this kind of thing, please know that you are most definitely not alone and that it takes a really brave person to come to terms with admitting it. How have you dealt with this pull to believe God loves others more than He loves you?

The Win/Win

We must come to terms with the truth that in God's economy, a win for one is a win for *all*. We're all on the same team. God never takes from one of His children to give to another. If you are struggling with the question of fair versus unfair, let me share with you a little secret that helped me a lot! God is not fair. Who ever told you He was? Our God is not fair—but He is *just*, and that's a much better thing for all of us!

Think about it. A fair God would be obligated to do the same thing in the same way at the same time for everyone. A just God gets to do what's best given each situation and each individual's uniqueness. As my dear friend, mentor, and hero John Lynch says, "God loves us equally, but He also loves us uniquely." I try to live by this as a mother of three children. I do my best to avoid being "fair" as their mom—meaning that if I do for one I have to do for all. What I try to do instead is to be the mom Amelia needs me to be for Amelia. The mom Macey needs me to be for Macey. And the mom Jackson needs me to be for Jackson.

There is only one you in this world. And God loves you in ways you can't even begin to fathom. He loves you enough to allow you to doubt His good character at times. He loves you enough to allow you to struggle in relationships while He is working in you, mending your heart and redeeming your skewed beliefs. God loves you enough to allow you to wonder about His love so that when you stumble into His vast and immeasurable love for you, you will be forever captivated by the One who is absolutely smitten with you.

And you know what? Most days, it is so much easier for me to tell you of this love than it is for me to believe it is true. This is one of the main purposes for the Church and one of the main reasons we're called into relationship: so that on those days or in those seasons when we struggle

> God loves us equally, but He also loves us uniquely.
>
> —John Lynch

to believe that this Love could really be trusted with our whole selves, with reckless abandon, someone would be there to remind us that it is. We need to be reminded often, and we need to be reminders for others, that our identity has already been determined by the One who loved us enough to die for us.

Equally but Uniquely Loved

I heard recently about a young bride who was stood up by her groom at the altar. My heart sank as I heard the story. Such rejection, abandonment, humiliation…not to mention the bills that would need to be paid even though her name did not change that day. My heart ached for the pain of that young woman. I could imagine the thoughts that tormented her heart and mind. *Why would God allow this to happen to me if He loves me?* It wasn't fair, was it?

But a few years later that same young woman walked toward the altar where her husband-to-be was waiting for her. God knew all along the path His child would need to take to get her to where she needed to be on that precise day, taking vows that would last her a lifetime. Our God loves us enough to allow us to travel a broken road and loves us enough to take each and every step right alongside of us. (And He knows where the road leads too!)

Thank God that He doesn't always give us what we want!

God is not Santa Claus. In no way is He obligated to prove His love for us by giving us everything we ask for. He loves us too much to do that! When we understand how much we are loved, we find ourselves in a unique position to accept God's gifts as He sees fit to give them—without falling into the trap of comparing our stories and situations with those of women around us.

Our mission? To accept and embrace God's love for us as unique individuals. We are on a tailor-made journey that places us in the best position to offer genuine and heartfelt love to others. It doesn't matter if they choose to show the same kindness to us or not. We have the power to accept others even if they don't have the ability to accept us in return.

When I speak at conferences about our tendency to believe in God's love for others more easily than we believe in His love for us, almost everyone acknowledges they're either dealing with this presently or have in the past. The enemy loves to trip us up in this area and will pull out all the stops to convince us that God's love isn't as big as the Bible says it is.

How has the enemy tried to convince you that God's love isn't big enough for you?

Personal Response

On a separate page, draw your own picture of God. What does this picture say about the way you understand and experience Him?

In Mary and Martha's story, which of the sisters do you most identify with and why?

Jesus's response to Martha was not one of anger or frustration, but of great love and concern. He was not telling her that her service didn't matter to Him; He was telling her that she mattered to Him even more than her service to Him. Sometimes, we as women, tend to find our value in what we can do rather than in who we are. How can you identify with this?

God has written an amazing love story to us. I'd like to invite you to take some time to write a love letter to Him today.

Dear heavenly Father, for this one reader who may be striving to believe but struggling to know that You really do love her, just as she is, and wherever she is, with all that she's done and all that's been done to her, would You boldly reveal Your matchless love to her in a personal way? Make the truth of John 3:16-18 come alive in her heart like never before. Thank You, God. In Jesus's name, amen.

3

Created for Relationship

Women speak two languages—one of which is verbal.
WILLIAM SHAKESPEARE

What If We Could Get This Right?

Several years ago, a study was published on the uniqueness of female friendships.[1] This study, along with several others, concluded that women are created with a biological need for connection with other women in a way that men are not, that we handle stress differently than men do, and that the quality of our friendships with other women is a determining factor to our overall health. This is a unique component of our female makeup. Without healthy relationships with other women, we are much more susceptible to illnesses and even premature death.

Think about your closest friendships. What makes friendships with other women different from your friendships with men?

I've heard it said that men connect shoulder to shoulder with other men and that women connect heart to heart with other women. (Perhaps this is why our feuds can get a little uglier and more personal than the guys'.) Life is richer when we have great friendships with other women. Whenever I'm dealing with something big, whether positive or negative, I always want to talk about it with one of my closest girlfriends. In 2004, Stephen and I dealt with the loss of two of our unborn children. I had miscarried in the first trimester two other times, but when I got to the second trimester with these two precious babies, I felt like I could breathe a sigh of relief—that the due date on the calendar would bring with it a healthy and dearly loved addition to our family. Unfortunately, that wasn't meant to be for either of those two pregnancies. I lost one baby at 13 weeks and the other, my daughter, at 15 weeks. In both of those seasons of grief, it was my girlfriends who most ministered to my heart. I'll never forget one friend in particular who called me during this time to see how I was. I couldn't even talk. All I could do was cry. So she didn't talk either. Every few seconds or so, I could hear her sobs on the other end of the line.

When my first book was published, on the other hand, I couldn't wait to share this good news with family and friends—and, of course, those women who had encouraged me through it all as I saw it come to completion.

> The best way to mend a broken heart is time and girlfriends.
>
> —Gwyneth Paltrow

It's just a fact: Close friendships make victory sweeter and loss easier to bear. It's easier to rejoice and to weep when you have a strong friend to draw on.

But in both these seasons for me, through the miscarriages and the publication of my book, I encountered people who could not bring themselves to offer comfort or joy. In fact, there were some who did the opposite and actually made belittling statements. I understand more clearly now that whenever a woman feels the need to offer cold-shoulder treatment to another woman, more than likely it is because she does not feel secure in how loved she is herself. (Remember the story of Mary and Martha?) She can't offer me what she doesn't realize she has a surplus of already. It is as though she is sitting on a gold mine but fearing she really lives on top of a graveyard. She's afraid to dig deep, fearing what she will uncover, and so never uncovers the treasure that is hers alone. How tragic. How unnecessary.

Baby, I was born this way...

No, really, I was! And you were too. Let me explain...

One major difference between men and women is the role that the hormone oxytocin plays in our lives and relationships. Oxytocin, sometimes referred to as the "bonding hormone," is found in both men and women and contributes

> Hold a true friend with both of your hands.
>
> —Nigerian Proverb

to feelings of trust and love between members of a couple, family, or "in-group." It is also part of what makes women bond differently with women than men do with men. Oxytocin is a hormone released when we nurse our infants, causing the mother-child bond to strengthen in intensity. Oxytocin "connects" us to others. I'm not a scientist, and I don't plan to turn this chapter into a biology lecture, but I did want to point this out to reveal yet another way that God designed us with not only a spiritual need for relationship, but with a biological need for connection.

Realizing this can make a world of difference in how we perceive our relationships with other women. Sure, guys need great relationships with other guys, but there is still something unique about how we as females were created and how our need is even more vital to our overall well-being.

A dear friend of mine, Dr. Brenda Wagner, tells me that female bonding is nothing new. You know what happens when women live together or work together often, don't you? Our bodies, for some reason, begin to "sync" with the other females' biological clocks. Over time, our monthly cycles begin to match. Dr. Wagner told me that years and years ago, before the modern conveniences we enjoy today were invented, "that time of the month" could really put a woman out of commission for a few days. So women in the same household or village—or the same tent in the desert—would be spending focused, uninterrupted time together every month. The result? A beautiful, sacred bond between women. (I would imagine, though, that because they were just as human as we are today, there might have been a few women in the tent who could have used this book!)

We need each other.

Understanding this reality was a catalyst which prompted me and a few other women to launch Church 4 Chicks in 2008. We knew we needed to create the space where these kinds of relationships could be cultivated. We each longed for a place that encouraged and helped to enrich genuine relationships among women. We didn't mind the tea parties and socials that we were mostly experiencing when it came to "women's ministry," but our hearts wanted something more, something that went deeper. We knew if we felt this way, others did too. And we were right. A lack of honest, authentic, and real relationships with other women is actually detrimental to my health and well-being! So it makes sense that if this is an area that is of such vital importance, our enemy would do his level best to make them as messy and miserable and conflicted as he can.

Think about that person you noted in Chapter One—the person you can't seem to get along with. Can you imagine how the enemy might be complicating matters in order to keep you from enjoying a peaceful relationship with each other? If so, how so?

Write down a prayer to your heavenly Father in regard to this matter.

Keys to Embracing Your New Identity

In 2003, my husband and I started taking a two-year class at our church for people who desired to be a part of the counseling ministry and for those already associated with it. Stephen signed up for it as a supplement to his seminary classes, as it was his goal to get an addiction recovery program up and running. I signed up as well, but I honestly had no idea why. All I knew then was that I sensed it was what God wanted me to do. Because I had gone through the pain of rejection and divorce, I found myself "counseling" other women who had experienced that same kind of loss. I guess I figured that God was going to use this class to better equip me for those conversations. But He had something much bigger in mind.

I thought I was there to learn how to help others, but what God wanted to do was to rescue me—from myself, from my past, and from a future I would never have grasped had I continued down the emotional path I was on at the time. It was during this two-year in-depth study that God clearly called me to ministry.

Our instructor, Reverend James Eubanks, started the two-year program off by spending the entire first semester studying the believer's identity in Christ. I heard things in that class that I had never been taught before—even though I had been in church my whole life. I want to share with you a few key truths, with his permission, that will help to guide us for the rest of our time together as we take steps toward greater peace in our lives and relationships.

As I've mentioned already, and want to reiterate: when you know who you are, you'll know what to do. Most people are struggling in the area of decision-making, handling crises, relating to others, parenting, budgeting, finances, and more because their foundation isn't based on the truth of who God says they are. If we are going to find peace within our relationships, it is going to be because we have come to embrace what God says is true about us and we have begun to live out of that reality. With this in mind, I want to pass along some key elements to understanding your identity as a child of God.

The Need for a God-Centered Approach to Life

Consider the following passages from the New Testament:

> For from him and through him and for him are all things.
> To him be the glory forever! Amen (Romans 11:36).

> For in him all things were created: things in heaven and on
> earth, visible and invisible, whether thrones or powers or
> rulers or authorities; all things have been created through
> him and for him (Colossians 1:16).

> When he has done this, then the Son himself will be made
> subject to him who put everything under him, so that God
> may be all in all (1 Corinthians 15:28).

It is vital that we view life through the filter of God's existence and His activity in the universe. Anytime I find myself struggling emotionally or grappling with anxious thoughts, I find that I have allowed *Shelley* to be the authority over my circumstances rather than God. When we view life through the lens of God's existence and character, it changes everything—even those relationships that are the most challenging to us. This is foundational. We must have this in place before we try to strategically build our lives.

This view changes everything. We begin to see the world and understand our experiences through the lens of eternity and not just the here and now. We begin to recognize God's fingerprints in the events and circumstances around us rather than thinking we're on our own. We begin to see that we can hang on to Him during the good times and the bad, understanding that His nature and character can be trusted even when circumstances try to prove otherwise. When we recognize that God is the source of life, and as we allow Him to be the center of our lives, we will find ourselves standing on a firm foundation. That foundation won't move, regardless of our day-to-day trials or the opinions of others.

This next one can be a bit tricky....

It Is in the Context of Relationships That God's Glory Is Made Known

The LORD God said, "It is not good for the man to be alone. I will make a helper suitable for him" (Genesis 2:18).

God is a relational being. God has always known and enjoyed relationship within the environment of the Trinity. Father, Son, and Spirit have always been fully God and fully unique personalities of the same God. Within that circle there has been a beautiful relationship filled with complete knowledge of one another, unity, love, fellowship, friendship, and purpose. If we lived in a perfect world, we would have experienced this kind of simplicity and wonder in our own relationships. But sin entered the picture, and that messed everything up! And wouldn't it make sense that if God designed us for relationship we would find some of the greatest opposition coming in this key area of our lives?

> As we receive (Agape) love from God, our role is to let it spill into the lives of others. By this God's love is made known.
>
> —Reverend James Eubanks, Director of Counseling, First Baptist Church, Woodstock, GA

The reality of sin, though, does not change God's design for you and for me. We are meant to exist in communion with one another! Jesus repeated this principle when He stated the Greatest Commandment in Matthew 22:37-39: "'Love the Lord your God with all your heart and with all your soul and with all your mind.' This is the first and greatest commandment. And the second is like it: '*Love your neighbor as yourself*'" (emphasis mine).

How is God's love made known?

Why do you suppose God chooses to make His love known in this way?

Scripture says that the highest goal is to love God and then love others as we love ourselves—not instead of ourselves. Most of us—if we are healthy—love ourselves: We feed our bodies, we clothe them, we allow them to rest and get sleep, we exercise our muscles, and so on. Loving others as ourselves means that God desires for our relationships to be full of health, vibrancy, and mutual respect and love for one another.

Confessions of a Former Mean Girl

When I was in sixth grade I was awkward and unpopular. Every day was traumatic for me. All of my elementary school years had been spent in a small, private, Christian school where at least one of my parents worked and where I felt some sense of belonging and security. But when I entered middle school, my parents put me, my older brothers, and younger sister in public school for the first time. I knew no one. I didn't know the social rules or how to act. I didn't listen to the same music the other kids listened to or watch the same TV shows and movies they watched. I didn't have the same clothes or sense of style as I was accustomed to uniforms.

It didn't take long, though, for me to find the one person who was a rung lower than me on the social ladder of success. I am embarrassed to admit how easily I took advantage of her. I should have risen up to show kindness and affirmation to her, especially after experiencing the same kind of treatment myself. But in order to make myself feel a little less shame and insecurity, I capitalized on her perceived inferiority. The truth is—and I hate to admit this—I didn't care one way or the other about her. I didn't see her as a person with a heart and soul. I only saw her as a means to an end, and I leveraged that opportunity for all its worth.

And I felt horrible about myself in the process. I can imagine her wondering, *What did I ever do to her?* To this day I remember her name and what she looked like. I remember the way I insulted her and I remember the embarrassment I caused her. It is one of those memories I wish I could erase so I wouldn't have to accept what I did. I look back and wish I could say, "The devil made me do it!" But I can't. I knew exactly what I was doing.

This experience, and its lingering memory, is another of the reasons this book exists. Not only have I dealt with people who didn't want to get along with me, but I've also been that difficult person for someone else. My behavior toward that poor girl was a result of my own faulty thinking and insecurity. Had I realized back then how loved I was and that God had created and designed me for relationship and to make His love known in the world, things would have been very different. Unfortunately, I didn't, but thankfully, God's grace is greater than all of this!

Why Can't We All Just Get Along?

So, if we were created for relationship by a relational Creator, why is it that we don't seem to be able to get along better with one another? Why are so many of our relationships left on a superficial level at best and a downright ugly level at worst? Why is it so easy to adopt a me-against-you or us-against-them attitude in life? Why do we give in to the pull to compare ourselves and our lives to every other female we come into contact with? And what is it about us girls that makes us so different from our male counterparts when it comes to relationships?

Why can't we all just get along?

When I was dealing with—for years and years—the relationship I mentioned in Chapter One, I didn't need another book full of pressure to be more and try harder. I needed something based on the gospel message—that because of Christ in me I would be able to experience the abundant life Jesus offers—where the peace of Christ could rule in my heart rather than allowing the fear of rejection or the pressure of insecurity to rule my thoughts, my emotions, or my actions. (See

Colossians 3:15.) I am confident that if you ask Him, God will meet you at your point of need.

So here's what we've figured out so far:

1. My understanding of my identity determines my behaviors and actions.

2. God created us for relationships.

3. It is in the context of relationships that His glory is made known here on the earth.

4. Jesus affirmed this truth when stating the Greatest Commandment.

5. There is something we can all do to experience greater peace even in the difficult relationships we face.

But this still begs the question: *How?*

Thankfully, the apostle Paul—someone who had his own share of difficult relationships—shared some very practical principles that, when applied

> You have failed to prove the sufficiency of God until you have asked of Him the impossible.
>
> —Anonymous

consistently, will help us learn how to relate in a healthier way with others and in the process find and experience lasting peace! In fact, in some cases, we'll find that the relationships that have been the most difficult become the very ones God uses to make His glory known as He heals old wounds and breathes life where there has only been death. Seem impossible? Well, that's okay. Our God delights in accomplishing what people deem impossible.

Personal Response

What idea or concept spoke to you most from this chapter?

Why do you think that is?

Do you believe relationships among followers of Christ should be healthier than those of non-believers? Explain your answer.

Dear heavenly Father, as we take these steps together reveal with compelling clarity how You see each and every one of us. Help us to see ourselves and those around us through the lens of Your grace and our identity. In Jesus's name, amen.

Part Two

When You Know Who You Are You Know What to Do

It's time to really get this ball rolling! In this next section we'll begin to unpack the six principles from Romans 12 that help us to do our part, that part that is totally up to us, to be at peace with everyone. Remember: When we know who we are, we'll know what to do. If we will all do our part, faithfully and consistently, fueled by whatever amount of trust we have in our trustworthy God, we'll begin to experience greater peace than ever—even in the relationships that have caused us the most anguish.

4

The Pressure Is Off!

"I have the right to do anything," you say—but not everything is beneficial. "I have the right to do anything"—but not everything is constructive.

<small>1 CORINTHIANS 10:23</small>

Have you ever felt like someone was trying to put you in your place? (That's a fun ride, huh?) I'll never forget a phone call I got several years ago. There was a woman in my life during that time who was on a mission to get me to give up the silly notion that God had a call on my life. Her reason: because I was in a second marriage. In her understanding of Scripture, I was now unfit for certain types of ministry because I had been divorced and was now remarried. At one point she actually said, "Shelley, think of what God *could have done* with your life if you had not made this mistake." She told me how much potential I had been given and how I had tied God's hands with my sinful choice to marry Stephen. I tried, for quite some time, to ask her if she could handle us disagreeing with each other without becoming disagreeable. But she was determined to get me to "repent so others don't make this same mistake."

What this woman was missing then, and I hope is not missing today, is that I am so much more than my marital status. In fact, I am so much more than my calling, my vocation, my educational level, my gender, or anything else that describes me. These labels may describe me, but they do not define me. Only God can do that. And only through an intimate relationship with Him based on His merits, His righteousness bestowed upon me, His grace, His favor, His will, and by His Spirit will I be able to move into the different phases of my life with confidence and assurance. This comes as I understand a very important reality: Because of my new nature, and because nothing can alter or change my identity once it has fused with the very nature of God Himself through Jesus Christ, I am now completely and utterly *free*. The apostle Paul, the great teacher of new identity and grace, dealt with this kind of thing in his day too as new Christians tried to police each other's behaviors and decisions, and he had a very simple, yet profound way to handle this that still applies to us today!

Permissible vs. Profitable

Paul affirmed that because of Christ and His righteousness, the pressure is off of our shoulders completely. Because we belong to Jesus, we do not have to do one single, solitary thing to earn our salvation. Jesus paid it all—completely. I *can* do anything, and my identity remains the same. God's love for me remains exactly the same because His love for me isn't based on my performance but on *His* identity. But although I *can* do anything, not all things are the best thing for me or for those whom God loves. God is love and He longs for us to embrace this part of the new nature He has placed within us.

As we look at these principles and begin to implement them in our lives, remember that this is not a "to do" list in order to please God or others. It's not a magic formula to fix all the broken relationships out there. The best way to view these principles is as helpful practices that we will implement because this is *best* for us and for those around us. If you never put any of these principles to work, God will still love you just as much as the person who implements them all perfectly. But if you do choose to cooperate with God's Spirit and His Word, you will be much better off because of it.

A living sacrifice? That sounds painful!

I don't know what your experience was like, but church has been a big part of my life for almost all of my life. I went to church nearly every time the doors were open until I was in middle school…which, come to think of it, probably had some effect on how I treated that poor girl back in the sixth grade! (Maybe the devil *did* make me do it! Yeah, right.)

> Therefore, I urge you, brothers and sisters, in view of God's mercy, to offer your bodies as a living sacrifice, holy and pleasing to God—this is your true and proper worship. Do not conform to the pattern of this world, but be transformed by the renewing of your mind. Then you will be able to test and approve what God's will is— his good, pleasing and perfect will (Romans 12:1-2).

Back in those early days, I rarely heard a Bible story that didn't include the technologically advanced use of visual aids known as the "flannel graph." Long before the days of video *everything*, those visual aids apparently did their job well. So many people who grew up going to Sunday School remember them and the stories they helped to illustrate.

Anytime there was a story about an animal sacrifice—a frequent topic in Old Testament literature—the little flannel cut-out depicting the lamb or bull being sacrificed always looked nice, clean, and even a little bit…happy? But as we can all imagine, Old Testament sacrifices were *nothing* like what we saw on those flannel graphs.

In 1992 I visited the Mayan Ruins in Mexico. After a long and bumpy ride away from most of civilization and into the jungle, we arrived at these amazing buildings constructed so long ago. The structures still left standing after hundreds of years were incredible to see with my own eyes. I tried to imagine the people who lived there—the families—the children. I wondered what every day must have been like for them in this paradise of a home, right by the ocean.

In front of one of the main temples we saw that day was a rectangular structure made of stone. Its four walls enclosed a fairly deep pit. I asked our tour guide what we were looking at, and he told me it was a sacrificial altar. I wondered what kinds of sacrifices they put on the altar and for what reason. I went back to my memories of flannel graphs with sheep or bulls or birds lying peacefully on the stone altars of biblical days. I was horrified at his reply.

Our guide told us that the Mayan people often went into battle against other groups of people nearby. Anytime they experienced victory, one soldier would stand out above all the rest as having been their "most valuable player," if you will. He was one who helped bring about their victory and was considered to be the best of the best. It was then this soldier's "honor" to offer himself as a sacrificial gift to their gods in gratitude for their benevolence. He would be burned alive on that altar as an offer of thanksgiving by his people to the "god" they worshipped. I could hardly wrap my mind around the story. It broke my heart that day, and it still breaks my heart today. This sacrificial system wasn't based on truth, but on what these people *believed* to be true. There's a huge difference.

To those of us who have never seen a sacrifice, let's just say we are fortunate. It's not a pretty sight. The closest I ever came to seeing anything even remotely close to an animal sacrifice was the day my dad cut off the heads of our chickens so we could have dinner. I'll spare you the gory details that kept me up many nights later. Just thinking back on it now sends a shiver up my spine.

Principle 1: Offer Yourself as a Living Sacrifice

This is a horrible idea to contemplate, so why would our God call us, ones He loves so much, to offer ourselves as living sacrifices?

Okay, I can imagine what you're thinking. "Shelley, I thought this chapter was called *The Pressure Is Off!* If God loves us so much, why would He call us to offer ourselves as living sacrifices? This seems like a contradiction." You're right. But sometimes we have to decide to lose a battle so that we can win the war. Let me explain...

To those who first read the letter, 2,000 years ago in Rome, this idea of a "living sacrifice" would have painted a powerful picture. No animal brought to the sacrificial altar made it out alive! The idea of a *living* sacrifice was a new idea. It was completely the opposite of what religious practice had always included: ugly, painful, bloody, gory death.

When you read the word *sacrifice*, what picture comes to your mind? (Feel free to draw or use words to describe the picture in your mind.)

I don't know about you, but when I read a book that claims it will help me live better, get better results than I'm currently getting, or enjoy life more, I don't just want to know that "what." I also want to know the "how." I get so frustrated when someone tries to tell me what I should be doing but fails to tell me how to do that very thing in real life.

Not only did the apostle Paul tell us the what—"Offer your bodies as a living sacrifice"—he also told us the "how" of implementing the principle. These aren't quick-fixes to all of our relationship struggles, but they are biblical principles that, when applied to our lives consistently over time, make a huge impact in every single facet of our personal experiences. God is a very organized and intentional being. He is of supreme intelligence, so there are valid, ironclad reasons for everything He instructs us to do.

The most important step of all, the one that will help us do all we can to be at peace with everyone, lays the only guaranteed foundation upon which to build our lives. Let's check Romans 12:2 together:

> Do not conform to the pattern of this world, but be transformed by the renewing of your mind. Then you will be able to test and approve what God's will is—his good, pleasing and perfect will.

This passage tells us:

Do not:

Do:

Explain briefly, and in your own words, how you can implement Principle 1 by applying this passage to your own life:

What does this Scripture verse say you will be equipped to do if you implement this practice to your life?

The very first element Paul mentions when telling the reader (us!) to offer themselves as living sacrifices is **to be intentional with God's Word.** It's important to remember that this instruction is based on the eleven chapters that came before it. Those chapters were full of teaching about who a Christian is as a result of their relationship with Christ. Because of the image of Christ within us, we can be renewed. How? By being intentional in our relationship with God's Word and allowing Him to transform us from the inside out.

A dead sacrifice does not have the capacity to think anymore, but a living sacrifice *does*. I can't become a living sacrifice if I don't give full and complete access of my thinking to God. This would be a frightening prospect if it weren't based on the character and nature of a loving God who delights in each and every one of us. Remember, *when you know who you are* (loved, valued, prized, cherished, redeemed, and saved) *you know what to do* (offer yourself as a living sacrifice by allowing God to transform the way you think).

God's Word Truly Is Alive and Powerful!

> For the word of God is alive and active. Sharper than any double-edged sword, it penetrates even to dividing soul and spirit, joints and marrow; it judges the thoughts and attitudes of the heart (Hebrews 4:12).

After reading the verse above, make a list of some of the attributes of God's Word in the space below:

God's Word goes far below the surface of any outward façade and penetrates where no person can. It reveals to us the motives, fears, and even faith that we may not have recognized in ourselves. It is the continued exposure to God's powerful and penetrating Word that transforms us from the inside out. This transformation process takes time, and it certainly isn't painless, but it is so worth it! Our personal peace and our success in relationships with others hinge on this very important truth. It is definitely worth our investment.

Conforming vs. Transforming

There is a difference between *conforming* and *being transformed*. Conforming is an external act. For example, if I conform to a certain group of people, I may begin to talk, act, dress, and even make decisions like they do. But I'll still be the same me on the inside. You probably have memories of a time in your life when you conformed to fit in with friends or people you hoped would accept you into their circle. But if I surrender to God, He will *transform* me from the inside out. Much like a caterpillar transforms into a butterfly, when we submit to God's purpose for our lives and His process of getting us there we find our true identity in each phase of the journey stays the same, and that maturity comes naturally as we rest in the truth of who God is and who He says we are.

According to (your understanding of) God's Word, who are you?

God's Word is powerful—penetrating even to our hidden thoughts and motives, revealing what we can't see about ourselves. God's Word acts as a surgeon's scalpel in the life of His child. Skillfully, and with great care, God gets down to the real issue and lovingly reveals and removes what can be damaging to the child He so dearly loves. God's Word is also a razor-sharp, double-edged weapon available to you and to me. Not only is God's Word the tool God uses to transform us, but He has also given it to us as a weapon for spiritual warfare. Although the devil does not make us do anything, we certainly don't want to minimize how much influence he has or how much he involves himself in our lives and in our relationships with others.

Ephesians 6:17 instructs us to "take…the sword of the Spirit, which is the word of God." In his book *Sparkling Gems from the Greek,* Rick Renner says that the sword in the verse isn't just a sword. "It is the Greek word *machaira*—a word that exacted fear in the minds of those who heard it! You see, this wasn't just a sword, but a weapon of murder that caused the victim horrid pain as he lay bleeding to death."[2] This weapon was used in close combat and often had a corkscrew-shaped end. It wasn't a sword to be used from a distance. It was one that had a very ugly purpose in mind for the one on the receiving end! In Rick Renner's words, "this one was a terror to the imagination!" This means that…

God's Word is an instrument of torture to the enemy of our souls!

As we practice this way of life—living out of the truths of God's Word and out of our true identity, we become powerful forces against the enemy's lies. Our struggle, says Paul in Ephesians 6:12, "is not against flesh and blood, but against the rulers, against the authorities, against the powers of this dark world and against the spiritual forces of evil in the heavenly realms." Our enemy is *not* the person who challenges us in life.

Making a priority of studying Scripture changes *us* from the inside out, helping us to live in freedom and leading us to lasting peace. We become bolder and far less easy to fool as God transforms our minds by His truth! And, as we'll see later, this place of freedom is what empowers us to confront those who come against us rather than continuing to allow the bitterness and tension to fester.

God's Word is where freedom is found.

> To the Jews who had believed him, Jesus said, "If you hold to my teaching, you are really my disciples. Then you will know the truth, and the truth will set you free" (John 8:31-32).

After reading the Scripture above, how would you define *freedom*?

God has given us the key to our own freedom. He doesn't hold freedom out in front of us like a dangled carrot in front of a mule, keeping us moving one step at a time toward His desired goal for us. He gives us the principles by which we can find and experience freedom—and then share that amazing information with others.

This passage is so powerful for me personally. I remember when it finally dawned on me that the truth itself will not set me free—but *knowing* the truth will! I was in yet another struggle with some different women in my life. I had tried to become friends with a particular group of women, and I had failed at every turn. I didn't understand why they didn't want to be my friend in return or what it was about me that they just didn't like. Rather than accept this and move on about my own business, I let the question and the rejection fester. Finally, after a very long time had gone by, I cried out to God that I was tired of this old battle, and wanted it to be over once and for all.

In my mind's eye, I could see myself in chains, held captive by an old wooden prison stock. I could see myself feeling tired, discouraged, and weary from having been there for so long. And then God showed me that those locks were not actually locked at all. Because of Christ's sacrifice, and the fact that I was a forgiven child of the Most High, I was no longer forced to remain in such bondage. I was there by my own lack of faith. God had *already* unlocked my chains and had *already* set me free. I just wasn't living in that freedom because I had become so accustomed to the bondage. God wanted me to understand in a way that my mind could comprehend the truth that would set me free. The truth was always the truth—but until I knew it for myself, I wasn't yet free.

We all have freedom etched on our hearts. We were created and designed to be free people. We long for it for a reason! Jesus spelled it out so clearly here for us. If we want to be free, we need to abide in God's Word. God knew we would be bombarded with lies constantly. He knew what a fierce battle we would face. The battle truly is in the mind! If we are going to have a chance at living as free women it is going to be through knowing and experiencing the truth, and the only way that will happen is if we surrender ourselves to be transformed by God's Word. When we choose to become serious students of the Bible, we put ourselves in the best position to embrace the truth God longs to reveal to us.

So the first and foundational step to living out of my true identity and doing all that is in my power to do to be at peace with everyone (Romans 12:18) is to be intentional with God's Word.

Personal Response

In what ways could you begin today to be more intentional with God's Word?

What would greater freedom look like in your life?

How willing are you to pursue freedom and peace?

Dear heavenly Father, open our eyes and our hearts to the eternally infinite love You have for us. As we receive this love from You—fully, humbly, gratefully, delightfully—let it spill over freely into the lives of others. In Jesus's name, amen.

5

Know Thyself

You can make more friends in two months by becoming genuinely interested in other people than you can in two years by trying to get other people interested in you.

DALE CARNEGIE

What was your first friendship with another female like? I can think back to my own. My best childhood friend was a girl named Danielle. Our parents served together at the church our families attended in Florida and we were together a lot.

Many of my earliest memories involve Danielle. She was three months older than me, and my mom credits her with getting me to walk when I was only eight months old. I guess I wanted to make sure I could keep up! When we were four years old, she taught me how to tie my shoes. And when *E.T.* came out—back when my family didn't go to movie theaters—she told me the whole story so I wouldn't feel left out. We were inseparable and loved being together. I felt safe with her and loved by her. And I guess, as a little girl, I thought it would always be this way.

Life Happens

My family moved away when Danielle and I were only eight years old. It was a very difficult transition for my whole family. And not long after we moved to Georgia I found out she had found another best friend. Although I couldn't blame her, the feeling of rejection and being easily replaced was painful. I learned through that experience that out of sight often means out of mind. Of course she did not intentionally hurt me, and it was something I was able to get over fairly quickly. But I still remember the hurt.

It wasn't what Danielle did that affected me so much; it was the meaning I gave to her actions. In my young, inexperienced, immature thinking and understanding, I attached a meaning to her behavior. Some of us have endured heart-wrenching experiences that far outweigh this childhood disappointment, but the issue is the same for us all. Whenever we experience rejection in life, and we will, we need to be aware of the meaning we take away from that rejection. Are we allowing it to determine our value and our worth? Are we holding someone and their acceptance of us in a too high (and possibly unhealthy) regard?

BFFs

I had other BFFs along the way through childhood and my teen years, and felt the sting of rejection and replacement again…and again…and again. I continued to attach meaning to these experiences. The meaning? That I was not worthy of being loved and that I needed to guard myself from ever allowing anyone (particularly a woman) from really getting to know me. I knew that if she saw the real me, she would reject me. I couldn't risk it. I'll never forget when I decided I would never give another female that title: Best Friend. It had taken on such a negative connotation that I decided I would never bestow it on another female. I kept women at arm's length, never letting anyone in all the way.

And I know I'm not alone in this.

In what ways have you attached meaning to the rejections you've dealt with in your life?

It's with this dynamic in mind that we go into the second part of Principle 1: "Offer myself as a living sacrifice." The first part, as you remember, is to be intentional with God's Word. The second part is what we'll discuss now.

Then What?

The second part of becoming a living sacrifice is found in Paul's admonition found in verse 3: "For by the grace given me I say to every one of you: Do not think of yourself more highly than you ought, but rather think of yourself with sober judgment, in accordance with the faith God has distributed to each of you."

I offer myself as a living sacrifice by (1) _____ _____ and (2) by *willingly* humbling myself before God and others.

Define humility in your own words:

Whenever I think of the word *humility*, I think of people I know who have displayed this rare quality in their everyday lives. I think of the women who serve alongside me at Church 4 Chicks. So much gets done behind the scenes that no one is even aware of, all because a few women are humbly going about their service without demanding that they be noticed.

One of the best examples of humility I know is the prophetess Deborah found in the book of Judges in the Old Testament. Deborah was one of the judges whom God raised up to lead

> Swallow your pride occasionally—it's nonfat!
> —Anonymous

His people during one of the many times they were caught up in the "try hard/give up cycle." You know what I mean, right? We decide we're going to get our acts together and do what's right, whether it is in the area of our health, nutrition, spiritual walk, job performance, studies, whatever... So, for a while we try really, really hard. But after a while fatigue or discouragement or boredom or illness sets in and we find ourselves with less energy to keep up the pace. So we give up...and for a while we feel better. That is, until the guilt sets in for not doing our part and not living up to our potential, or whatever it is that motivates guilty feelings within us. So, we hop back on the treadmill and we start again. Try hard. Give up.

This is what the Israelites were experiencing. God had shown them His grace and mercy and power, and the people tried hard for a while, but then they'd give up. They would not just give up, though—they would start doing all sorts of awful things to one another.

I teach my children that if they can learn to be successful in their relationships, they can be successful in life. The opposite also holds true. Show me a person who is unsuccessful relationally, and I'll show you a person who can't get a handle on their work, their health, or their life in general. We see this played out again and again in the story of God's people. As the Israelites moved further from God, they began to treat one another in less than honorable ways. Their relationships were suffering big time. So God called certain men and certain women to be judges of His people to help guide them and help them handle their disputes. Enter Deborah.

> Again the Israelites did evil in the eyes of the LORD, now
> that Ehud was dead. So the LORD sold them into the hands
> of Jabin king of Canaan, who reigned in Hazor. Sisera, the
> commander of his army, was based in Harosheth Hag-
> goyim. Because he had nine hundred chariots fitted with
> iron and had cruelly oppressed the Israelites for twenty
> years, they cried to the LORD for help. Now Deborah, a
> prophet, the wife of Lappidoth, was leading Israel at that
> time. She held court under the Palm of Deborah between
> Ramah and Bethel in the hill country of Ephraim, and
> the Israelites went up to her to have their disputes decided
> (Judges 4:1-5).

The story of Deborah's leadership of Israel goes on to reveal a quiet
confidence about her that reflects a heart of genuine humility. I so want
this trait to be true of me! She was a strong, bold, courageous woman
who was confident in who she was and in what she was called to do.
Because she knew who she was, she knew what to do. Her reputation
brought courage to others as well! Just read what the Bible records of
an instance that verifies this:

> She sent for Barak son of Abinoam from Kedesh in Naph-
> tali and said to him, "The LORD, the God of Israel, com-
> mands you: 'Go, take with you ten thousand men of
> Naphtali and Zebulun and lead them up to Mount Tabor. I
> will lead Sisera, the commander of Jabin's army, with his
> chariots and his troops to the Kishon River and give him
> into your hands.'" Barak said to her, "If you go with me, I
> will go; but if you don't go with me, I will not go" (verses
> 6-8).

Do you see the significance here? Deborah sends an officer into
battle with orders and he insists that she come with him! This woman
commanded honor and respect. Anyone who thinks humility has to
look like weakness or self-hatred, as my mom would say, "has another
think coming!"

Quiet Confidence

As we consider this quality, one that our Lord Jesus Christ displayed so perfectly, I want us to clarify its meaning so that we can understand the difference between genuine and healthy humility and false, unhealthy humility. We've all known someone who pretended to be humble to the point that it made us sick, right? So let's look at this for a few minutes together, shall we?

Humility is not...

Let's first discuss what humility is *not*. Humility is not thinking poorly of yourself. Due to the different experiences with rejection I experienced as a child, like when my BFF moved on so quickly, and other, even more painful times I felt that awful sting, I adopted a shame-based (false) view of myself rather than a humble (accurate) view of who I was. When we attach false meaning to real experiences, we adopt an unhealthy view of life in general. Everything gets colored by that meaning we've attached to our experiences. When we see ourselves and assess life through the lens of shame, it distorts every single thing. We can think we are just being humble when we put ourselves down, expect the worst thing to happen to us, or adopt a griping, complaining attitude, but show me where Jesus displayed these behaviors.

The most honestly humble people you'll meet are the ones who have the healthiest concept of who they are. They don't see themselves as better than other people, but neither do they see themselves as worse than others. They view themselves through God's assessment and allow Him to be the final authority—not other flawed beings. Consequently, genuinely humble people enjoy genuinely healthy relationships.

You can be a confident, bold, courageous, and wild woman of God, like Deborah, and still have the humility of Christ working actively in you. In fact, if you have the humility of Christ working in you, you will be a confident, bold, courageous, wild woman of God! It's a natural byproduct of genuine, Christ-produced humility in the life of a daughter of God. It is absolutely vital for us to have a proper and true view of who we are. In doing so, we open ourselves up to accepting and appreciating the differences we see in others in a spirit of honest humility. (We get to dive into this part in the coming chapters!)

How do you feel when someone in your life "fishes for compliments"?

Why do you think they do this?

Before we move on...

For some people, humility is understood to be an attribute by which one scolds herself (whether privately or publicly), demeans herself and her contributions in front of others, negates God's work of redemption in her life by constantly criticizing herself, and compares herself incessantly to others. This attitude can become so ingrained that a woman will beg for your affirmation even as she belittles herself. No one wants to believe the worst about herself, but for some it has become a way of thinking and speaking. Most people, I'd say, don't even realize they're doing it.

False humility can become an addiction. When we crave the acceptance and affirmation of others to the point that we have to have it to be okay, we find ourselves on a slippery slope and others at a dead end. No one can fill up the "acceptance tank" of another person completely. It wasn't what we were created to do. It is not pleasant to be around someone who displays this degree of false humility for very long. In their quest for praise, they tend to get the opposite of what they desire. They want affirmation and acceptance and approval, but more often than not they repel the very people whose opinions mean the most to them. It is a heavy weight to carry for both people in a relationship.

It can be so painful but so very freeing when we see this issue in ourselves and acknowledge it for what it is. Remember that every time Jesus connected or communicated with anyone, He did so with their history in mind. He knows your story too. He knows how you adopted a shame-based view of yourself. If you see yourself in what has just been shared, take a deep breath and talk to your heavenly Father about this. He longs for you to be free indeed!

Humility is…

So if humility doesn't mean shame, what does it mean? Humility is having a proper estimation of yourself based on what God says of you. It puts the focus on who God is and who He is in you, rather than on you on your own. Humility acknowledges that God is who He says He is and that you are who He says you are. No more. No less.

Humility is a choice we make, *not* a personality trait. No one is born humble! We have to be intentional to go to God's Word to get the picture of who we are and where we are in our journey with Him, receiving God's correction, instruction, and edification. Because God knows how dangerous pride is to you, to those around you, and to the kingdom, He will take it upon Himself to humble you when necessary. He deems you worth it because He knows it is the best thing for you.

Humility attracts God's grace. James 4:6 teaches that God opposes or resists the proud, but He gives grace and shows favor to the humble. That's reason enough for me to put this principle into practice. I don't know about you (actually I do—we're all in the same boat), but I am desperately in need of His grace every moment of every day!

Consider what Scripture has to say about humbling ourselves:

- Humble yourselves, therefore, under God's mighty hand, that he may lift you up in due time (1 Peter 5:6).

- Wisdom's instruction is to fear the LORD, and humility comes before honor (Proverbs 15:33).

- Before a downfall the heart is haughty, but humility comes before honor (Proverbs 18:12).

Let's face it, humility is an area we all need help with, right? The opposite of humility is pride or arrogance, and it's always easier to see in others than ourselves. I believe that if we choose to be intentional with the first part of this principle, being intentional with God's Word, we will find ourselves maturing in this vital area of spiritual growth. And if the goal is to be humble, I'd much rather humble myself than have to wait for God to do it for me! Wouldn't you?

Remember, when you know who you are and have a healthy view of yourself in light of Christ in you, then you will know what to do. Most people in the Church today would not be able to tell you what it means to have Christ in them, and yet, according to the New Testament, this is foundational to successful living!

Personal Response

What is the first principle for doing all that you can to live at peace with everyone?

What are the two parts that make up this principle?

What will you do today to begin to implement these biblical principles into your life?

Is there a relationship you are currently concerned about? If so, how might this principle of "offering yourself as a living sacrifice" make a difference in how you move forward in your interactions with that person?

Do you know someone who displays the qualities described as genuine humility or quiet confidence? Describe this person. (Hint: If you just described yourself, you might want to re-read this chapter again. Just sayin'!)

Dear heavenly Father, thank You so much for the promise that we are not on this journey alone. Not only do You remain with us at each and every stop and start, You also send others into our lives to walk with us. For those times when we can't feel You near us, I pray that we will trust that your presence remains— always. Forever. Eternally. And for those times when we find ourselves doubting, help our unbelief. Show us who we can encourage to believe today. In Jesus's name, amen.

Check out more from Shelley at
www.shelleyhendrix.org/2012/03/be-who-you-really-are.html

6

Big Girls *Do* Cry

Much of the vitality in a friendship lies in the honoring of differences, not simply in the enjoyment of similarities.

UNKNOWN

When I was a teenager I dated a guy whose mom, for whatever reason, did not like me. She didn't even try to pretend that she did. I wanted so much for her to like me and I tried everything I could think of to win her over, but she would not give me a chance. I'll never forget the conversation I had with the guy after I had spent the day with his family. I had hoped that maybe once she spent a little time with me she would change her mind about me. I was wrong.

My boyfriend told me that his mom felt like I was ungrateful because, according to her, I had never thanked her for the lunch she made for our picnic. Now, I can be accused of a lot of things, but not thanking someone ain't one of them! In our house, you said please and thank you for everything. And I do mean *everything*. There were four of us kids in my family and we can all remember hearing our parents saying, over and over again, "What do you say?" That was the cue for a please or thank you!

So when I was accused of being ungrateful, I'll just tell you right here and now, I was ticked! I knew that I knew that I *knew* that I had thanked that woman for the peanut butter and jelly sandwich at least a half a dozen times. I thanked her for allowing me to hang out with them. I thanked her for letting me attend the event they went to. I probably thanked her for saying hello to me and good-bye when I left. I knew I had thanked her. Apparently after that conversation, he had a little talk with his mom. The next time this came up he said, "I told her what you said and reminded her that you did say thank you. She said, 'Well, she didn't say it enough.'" I'm not with that guy anymore.

"Unexpressed gratitude communicates ingratitude."[3] I can be grateful for my husband and what he does for me and our family and in the lives of others all day long and twice on Sunday, but if I never express it, then to him I would appear to be one very ungrateful chick indeed! I think that one of the reasons we have such a hard time getting along with certain people—or perhaps why they have such a hard time getting along with us—is because we either don't appreciate one another for who and how God made us or we have failed to express it to them… or else they have failed to express their gratitude to us.

Who needs to hear you say thank you today? Go for it before you proceed.

God not only created us for relationship for the sake of learning and growing in our knowledge of His love for us and others, but so that, together, we would be more effective in this world than we would be on our own. I'm a pretty efficient gal when I put my mind to it, but I can always get much more accomplished when I invite the input, resources, knowledge, and participation of others. It is true that you might be able to go faster alone, but you will never go as far as you are capable of going

> Shared joy is a doubled joy. Shared sorrow is half a sorrow.
>
> —Swedish Proverb

unless you are part of a team heading in the same direction and headed toward the same goal.

Several years ago I had a great idea. I tell you this because I don't have great ideas every day. I don't even have great ideas every *month*! Do you remember Lisa Welchel's character, Blair Warner, on the 80s TV show *The Facts of Life*? I can still hear her say, "I just had another one of my *brrriiillliiiaaannntt* ideas!" Well, that is not me, so when it is my turn to have a great idea, I get pretty excited about it.

I was helping out as a behind-the-scenes volunteer at a ministry I was involved with in my twenties. I loved meeting the other volunteers and seeing the final results when the plans and preparations all came together and the attendees were impacted through our efforts. This was around the time when I had that great idea I just mentioned. It was about an event I thought would be really meaningful to those who regularly attended and would also bring in some new faces that we could potentially reach for the first time with the message of Jesus Christ. I couldn't wait to share it with the team leader! I just knew she was going to love the idea too.

I shared it with her and at first she seemed mildly interested, but I didn't see it going anywhere after a while. She said they had tried that kind of idea in the past but it didn't catch any wind under it, so they put it on the back burner. I wasn't devastated, but I was a bit disappointed. After all, it was a great idea. And like I said, I don't get those that often.

Fast forward a few weeks and I'm in a room with the team leader and a few others when she decides to share *her* great idea with them—the exact idea I had shared with her. She said the wheels were already in motion and the event was on the calendar. I couldn't believe it.

I never said anything about it to her or anyone else involved. The idea turned out to be a really great idea after all. It was a very nice event and many lives were touched—including my own. But it didn't minimize the hurt and disappointment I felt when I was never acknowledged for the idea I shared or the part I played in helping to make the event happen in the first place. And the lack of acknowledgment didn't hurt nearly as much as the betrayal I felt from the team leader.

The truth is, maybe she felt grateful. Maybe she meant to let others

know that I had come up with the idea. Maybe she meant to thank me.
Maybe her parents didn't brainwash her the
way my parents brainwashed me and my
siblings. Maybe she forgot I had shared the
idea with her. Maybe not. I may never
know, but what I do know is this: If we
want to get along with others, if we want to
do our part in being at peace with everyone, we need to realize that in
the big picture of life, it ain't all about us, sister!

> Silent gratitude isn't much use to anyone.
> —G.B. Stern

   I'm thankful that I had at least enough foresight to know I didn't
need to let this kind of thing eat me up. I don't know what compelled
the team leader to take the credit for the idea. I decided maybe she
needed it more than I did. Most likely, she was looking for validation
based on how she performed as a ministry leader rather than on who
she was because of Christ in her. I'm also glad that God spoke to my
heart through this whole ordeal and helped me grow through it, painful and disappointing as it was. He wastes nothing.

   I share this with you now because it is important for us to realize
that we are all, in some way or another, connected to one another—
and for a reason. If we're to do our part to get along with others—to
be at peace with everyone—then we need to learn the importance
of accepting and appreciating the differences we see in others—and
acknowledging those from time to time.

> In this way we are like the various parts of a human body.
> Each part gets its meaning from the body as a whole, not
> the other way around. The body we're talking about is
> Christ's body of chosen people. Each of us finds our mean-
> ing and function as a part of his body. But as a chopped-off
> finger or cut-off toe we wouldn't amount to much, would
> we? So since we find ourselves fashioned into all these excel-
> lently formed and marvelously functioning parts in Christ's
> body, let's just go ahead and be what we were made to be,
> without enviously or pridefully comparing ourselves with
> each other, or trying to be something we aren't (Romans
> 12:4-6 MSG).

Have you ever had an experience with someone taking the credit or affirmation that was rightfully yours? How does the Scripture passage above apply to that situation?

This takes us to our next principle...

Principle 2: Accept and Appreciate the Differences You See in Others

Before we talk about how incredible our differences really make us and why this is such an over-the-top wonderful gift to humanity, let's first deal with something that is definitely not an issue that only affects us women, shall we?

Several years ago I was reading through Paul's letters throughout the New Testament. I imagined myself in situations he found himself in, chills running down my spine as I visualized the many dangers he faced. It makes me wonder how anyone could believe Christianity to be a false religion after taking an honest look at the life-change of Saul of Tarsus to Paul the apostle! Talk about a 180-degree turnaround! And yet with all the dangers he faced—shipwrecks, stoning, snakebites, long-term stays in dungeons and prisons—none of it seemed to ruffle his feathers as much as the conflicts among believers did.

Take a look at Philippians 4:2-3: "I plead with Euodia and I plead with Syntyche to be of the same mind in the Lord. Yes, and I ask you, my true companion, help these women since they have contended at my side in the cause of the gospel." Paul must have wondered as he heard about the dissension between these two women, "Why can't we all just get along?"

Recently, while on a short-term mission trip, I met a pastor in his fifties who shared with our team how he came to become a pastor. He said that his call to ministry was a big surprise to him—he never saw that as a potential career path for his life. He also shared with us that shortly after he surrendered to this call to become a pastor, his four-year-old son died suddenly in a drowning accident while he and his family were on vacation. My heart sank inside of me when I heard him tell the story. I've experienced pregnancy loss four times, and those losses almost sunk me. I cannot even begin to imagine the loss of a child who has become a daily part of my life and family. What he said next, though, was what stunned me most and what continues to play over and over in my mind: "Losing our son was nearly unbearable for my wife and me. We didn't know how we were going to get through it. I preached my first sermon twelve days after he died. But you know, people think that the hardest thing to go through in this life is the death of a child. And as unbearably painful as that is to go through, it is not the most painful thing. The hardest thing to deal with is the wounds that Christians inflict upon one another."

Ouch.

What is your response to this pastor's statement?

In what ways do we as believers wound one another?

Why do you think we do this?

What is lost when believers are not "of the same mind in the Lord" for the sake of the gospel?

In the book of Philippians, Paul shares some insight into this kind of issue—he had the whole "Why can't we all just get along?" thing *down*. He had learned a lot by this point and so we are wise to pay attention to his sage advice. Read the passage here and then we'll continue with this thought:

> Now I want you to know, brothers and sisters, that what has happened to me has actually served to advance the gospel. As a result, it has become clear throughout the whole palace guard and to everyone else that I am in chains for Christ. And because of my chains, most of the brothers and sister have become confident in the Lord and dare all the more to proclaim the gospel without fear. It is true that some preach Christ out of envy and rivalry, but others out of goodwill. The latter do so out of love, knowing that I am put here for the defense of the gospel. The former preach Christ out of selfish ambition, not sincerely, supposing that they can stir up trouble for me while I am in chains. But what does it matter? The important thing is that in every way, whether from false motives or true, Christ is preached. And because of this I rejoice (Philippians 1:12-18).

Or in other words...

> It's true that some here preach Christ because with me out of the way, they think they'll step right into the spotlight. But the others do it with the best heart in the world. One group is motivated by pure love, knowing that I am here defending the Message, wanting to help. The others, now that I'm out of the picture, are merely greedy, hoping to get

something out of it for themselves. Their motives are bad. They see me as their competition, and so the worse it goes for me, the better—they think—for them. So how am I to respond? I've decided that I really don't care about their motives, whether mixed, bad, or indifferent. Every time one of them opens his mouth, Christ is proclaimed, so I just cheer them on (Philippians 1:15-18 msg)!

I was a bit surprised when I realized that Paul—a guy—dealt with some of the same relationship realities that we as females do. The lesson I learned here continues to stay with me—even to this very day. Paul reveals in a clear way that we all deal with difficult people and that we all have a choice in how we respond.

Critic, Cynic, Competitor?

I have found that people tend to be critics, cynics, competitors, or... something else. We'll get to that in a bit. All of these three categories are found in dysfunctional relationships. This can be seen anywhere you have people together. It is unfortunate that they occur at all, but it is devastating to find these attitudes so prevalent within the family of God. Criticism, cynicism, and competition don't belong, but we find them everywhere we look.

The Critic

The critic is a person who judges, evaluates, or criticizes. It is also a person who tends too readily to make harsh or trivial judgments. She finds faults in everything. The critic is that person who will look for every little flaw in order to tear down the person she sees as inferior to her or in competition with her...or maybe even the person she feels threatened by. Often, she doesn't understand that's where her criticism is coming from.

You've probably met plenty of critics in your own life and have experienced hurt at their hands, but here's one example I heard recently:

"God has taught me through others that my strength comes through words. My mother's tongue was as sharp as a double-edged sword and she could fillet me up quicker than anyone I know...I believed that my mother didn't love me for who I was. I believed that she didn't support me or believe in me. She was my dream slayer. She never praised any of my accomplishments."

These words came from a comment posted on my blog when I asked readers to share some of their experiences in handling difficult relationships. The brief story told here is manifested and multiplied in different ways all over the world—right now. Critics can make their targets feel worthless and discouraged. The power of life and death truly is in the tongue, and we need to be cautious in words we offer and in words we listen to and allow to take up root in our minds.

Here's another example of a critic: A teenage girl I know liked wearing her eye makeup in a fashionable way, but that didn't sit well with her grandmother. Instead of choosing to offer positive feedback to her granddaughter or simply to choose to follow the old adage, "If you can't say something nice, don't say anything at all," the grandmother told her she looked like a devil worshipper. Way to go, Grandma. Not only was this completely unnecessary, but it was also hurtful for no reason.

Critical people don't just happen. Somewhere along the lines, they began to feel a strong urge and compulsion to be in control, to be right, to be validated. Their criticism is motivated by fear. It stems from a place of unresolved brokenness and when it continues to go unresolved, everyone—including the critic—suffers for it. They fear acknowledging that another person could be right, good, and valuable when they say or do things differently from them. Wouldn't that make them *wrong?* Think about the woman who constantly wants to tell you how she raised her children and how you need to do it just like her.

Have you encountered a critic? How do you deal with the difficulties that arise as a result of that person's criticism of you?

If fear is driving her behaviors, what would be the cure to her critical spirit?

The Cynic

The cynic is a person who is bitter, distrustful, contemptuous, or pessimistic. She's always questioning your motives. This is the person who expects you to fail and doesn't hesitate in making her opinion known.

Just think of the last time you decided you were going to get healthier, start an exercise program, and lose weight. The cynic was the one telling you how she tried that and it didn't work…and how it won't work for you either. Or that time your child was struggling in some way. The cynic was the one telling why you were going about everything wrong and how you didn't parent that child right anyway so now she'll never measure up. Sometimes cynics don't come right out and say this, but they definitely get their opinion across in obvious ways, don't they? They don't just measure you by your actions, they see themselves as the authority on your motives as well—and they don't usually give you the benefit of the doubt.

I experienced this a lot as I began to make it known that God had called me to ministry and that I was feebly taking steps to follow Him on this unfamiliar path. I was already having a really hard time believing God would want to use me in any kind of significant way at all. I dealt with one insecurity after another, but little by little trusted God and took steps of obedience toward the call on my life.

At one point, I was asking for advice from a friend about getting something on paper to give to churches and event planners who might invite me to come speak for them. I really had no idea what would be proper and so I was seeking counsel from folks who knew more than me. This was completely out of my comfort zone as it was and I was taking a risk of looking foolish in even asking the question. Out of the other room comes a woman who couldn't resist saying, "Don't you think you might be getting ahead of yourself? You don't even know

before, so why bother? I'm not exaggerating or taking dramatic license. She tried to convince me—still before the class had even begun yet— that if I did not have a certain number of women in the class on the first day, there was no point in even having the class. You needed a certain number to make it worthwhile, after all.

I told her that I knew God had called me to lead this study and that even if no one else showed up I was supposed to be there. I also wanted her to know she was under no obligation to stay and it would not offend or upset me in the least if she wanted to go to another class.

People did eventually show up, and after we had had a few sessions God began to stir my heart in very specific ways as He revealed a call to ministry on my life. I did not share this with the class, but I knew God was going to begin opening doors for me to speak and to teach. There was great connection being made among the women in that small group and our connection was growing. As more and more women began attending and God's call was becoming a certainty in my life, that same woman returned to let me know how many churches she had spoken at and how much more qualified she was to speak and to teach. She had to tell me how "brilliant" others said she was in her writing and speaking and ministry leadership and how I probably shouldn't bother because I didn't have her education, experience, or marital success. You see I had been married previously, went through a painful, unwanted divorce, and was remarried to another man (my husband, Stephen). She said I had missed God's mark and that it was such a shame that God would never be able to use me "like He wanted to" before I had messed up so much by marrying another man.

If I had a dime for every time this woman told me how highly others spoke of her, I could probably take you and me both to Disney World for a week. I *can't* do that, but what I got was of even greater value. God taught me a lot through that experience. One thing was that God loves me and has a great plan for my life, and another thing was that when He is actively working in my life, the enemy will intensify his own strategy to fuel *his* plan for my life as well. But that's okay... God is bigger and stronger than all the Goliaths put together.

Ever feel the pull to enter into competition with someone who is supposed to be on the same team as you? Describe your experiences with this here:

In the next chapter, we'll look at the antidote to allowing ourselves to give in to the pull to behave as a critic, cynic, or competitor with other women. It's so freeing to lay down those burdens and walk away in freedom, taking this message to others who have been held captive for far too long.

Personal Response

Write out Principle 2 here:

When you think about women you've most struggled with in the past, or struggle with today, what emotional response do you typically feel? How long does that emotional response usually last?

Why do we allow ourselves to get so emotionally, mentally, and spiritually wrapped up in what others do or don't do? (In other words, why do we give so much power to other people?)

What could be different about our interactions with difficult people in our lives if we remembered our own identity is based on Christ in us and not on what any other person thinks, views, believes, or likes/dislikes about us? How might this help us to accept and appreciate our differences?

Dear heavenly Father, give us wisdom and a clear vision to understand that we all behave out of our woundedness. As we receive Your grace for ourselves, make us mighty conduits of grace to others who so desperately need it. In Jesus's name, amen.

7

Pom-Poms Are
One-Size-Fits-All

Next to the wound, what women make best is the bandage.
JULES BARBEY D'AUREVILLY

I wasn't a cheerleader growing up. I toyed with the idea from time
to time, but due to lack of funds, my parents' busy work schedules, and
my own lack of balance and coordination, I never got to don the pom-
poms to cheer the home team on.

Why do you think sports teams choose to have cheerleaders at their
games?

Everyone needs people who are willing to cheer them on in life,
don't they? There is something special about the camaraderie of being
part of a team where everyone wears the same jersey and everyone is in
sync with one another, unified for a common cause. This goes beyond
our favorite college football teams (Go Dawgs!) and into our lives. We

all want to feel like we are a part of something bigger than ourselves. We want to belong.

As I mentioned before, I figured that the whole dynamic of comparison, criticism, cynicism, and competition that we discussed in the last chapter was probably pretty much a "girl thing" until I realized that Paul the apostle experienced some of this as well. In Philippians 1 Paul talks about how there were other teachers who made themselves Paul's competitors—all on their own. This wasn't something God put into place. God doesn't work that way, and neither did Paul. He set such a great example to us all. I love how Paul responded to this when it happened to him:

> So how am I to respond? I've decided that I really don't care about their motives, whether mixed, bad, or indifferent. Every time one of them opens his mouth, Christ is proclaimed, so I just cheer them on! (Philippians 1:18 MSG).

Paul, who also wrote the book of Romans, shared a power-packed principle for dealing with the critics, the cynics, and the competitors. He decided to be their biggest cheerleader!

Born for This!

I don't know about you, but I definitely do not want to be a critic, a cynic, or a competitor with my brothers and sisters in Christ. I've come to appreciate that a win for one of us is a win for all of us! We're all on the same team. We wear the same jersey, so to speak. And you know what? God doesn't take from one of us to give to another. However, we often act like this is the case. Deep down we think He's holding out on us.

The basic motivating force behind the behaviors of the Critic, the Cynic, and the Competitor is hidden shame. Shame that has her bound up in fear that her life isn't as valuable as yours and that if she allows herself to show you grace, she will lose even more than she has already lost. Whereas feelings of guilt spring from my actions, attitudes, or behaviors, feelings of shame spring from my beliefs about *myself*.

These critics, cynics, and competitors do not need our sarcasm. They don't even need our pity. They need *grace*. The same grace that you and I need every single day.

Pom-Poms Are One-Size-Fits-All

By God's matchless grace, I get to be a cheerleader for others! I mentioned at the beginning of this chapter that I didn't get to be a cheerleader growing up. But that's okay. I can be a cheerleader for the rest of my life and it isn't contingent on finances, schedules, or even my balance and coordination. It is my role and privilege to encourage others—you!—on to follow the dreams God has placed within them (you!); knowing that in God's goodness He isn't going to leave me out altogether! He has something supernatural and significant for me as well—something personal between Him and me. That is what I want!

When I become cynical, critical, or competitive, no one gets to enjoy the victories as much because even those become tainted by jealousy, bitterness, or envy. When I cheer you on, celebrating your victories with you, we all win!

> But encourage one another daily, as long as it is called "Today" (Hebrews 3:13).

I mentioned that I have had some wonderful encouragers in my life. I want to share a story with you about one fantastic and wonderful cheerleader God brought into my life just a few years ago. Now this woman could easily have set herself up as any of the first three types of women. She is more educated than I am with more accolades to her name, so being my Critic would have been effortless for her. She has written more books and spoken to more people. At the time, I only had one *self-published* book out in the market. Being cynical of me would have been easy. Her ministry platform is larger and more influential than mine, so if she wanted to be my competitor she'd win hands down. But instead, this amazing woman has chosen to be my friend, my encourager, and one of my biggest cheerleaders.

I'll never forget something she told me when our friendship first formed. We were both speaking at a conference and because we were not the keynote speakers, we had a little more downtime than usual. This was totally a God-thing. That weekend is full of great memories in large part due to her presence in it.

We ate lunch together and she asked me about the ministry, where I saw myself in a few years, and what I sensed God was up to in my life and this ministry. I was shy to share with her. Like I said, I've had really hurtful things said and done to me by other women who could have been cheering me on to follow God, but chose instead to tear me down. I shared a little with her to answer her questions, and her reply was overflowing with grace and kindness.

She told me about people she'd like to connect me with who could help me pursue God's call. She encouraged my dreams and affirmed my journey. In my surprise and delight I told her how unexpected this kind of response was after all the negative experiences I had had up to that point. And she simply said, "Shelley, sometimes God allows one of His kids to get ahead of another so that she'll be in a good position to open the door." I was and still am absolutely amazed by that statement. *That*, my friend is a Cheerleader, and it is my sincere hope to be that person for as many people as I can possibly be in my lifetime.

Do you have any cheerleaders in your life? Jot down a few of their attributes and actions.

Has anyone come to your mind who might be in need of a cheerleader to help her have courage to follow God's direction in her life? Who is this and how will you cheer her on?

Introvert or Extrovert?

Sometimes all it takes to be better equipped to cheer someone else on in her journey is to take a long enough pause to allow ourselves time to discover the beauty in how God made others. For example, I am very extroverted. This can drive quiet, pensive introverts to the edge! I've also been known to allow the differences in my introverted husband to bother me instead of recognizing that his needs for quiet, consistency, and planned-out events versus full-on spontaneity are a part of how God made him.

Many times, rather than cheering someone on to run down the path God has placed her on, we instead try to cheer them over to our path—to be more like us, be passionate about what we are passionate about, to embrace a life view we have adopted, to parent like we parent, to enjoy free time the way we enjoy it, to champion the causes that have gripped us. But what could happen if instead we allowed, supported, and encouraged the other people in our lives (especially our children) to go full-on after the thing God has tailor-designed them to do? What might happen if we decide to stop trying to make other people become more like us?

Is there someone in your life who needs to hear you cheer her on to be who God made her to be and to do what God has made her to do? Before you move on, go ahead and address this. This could be an incredible turning point for both of you.

Wherever You Go, There You Are

Wherever you find yourself today, critic, cynic, competitor, or cheerleader, know that God sees you, and God cares. He knows the journey you have been on, and perhaps has brought you to this book and this chapter for such a time as this, so that with Him you can finally deal with this head on. I can handle constructive criticism or confrontation so much better when I know the person giving it is *for* me. There is no one more for you and for me than God. His discipline is never to punish us but to build us up; never to push us away until we get our act together, but to draw us in so that He can help us grow. As my friends at TrueFaced say, "God speaks with one voice"[4] and that voice is always one of love, grace, and truth.

In some instances, we find ourselves easily cheering on one person while competing with another. Or cheering one person on while criticizing another. Take some time to allow the Father to do some heart work to uncover where these motives and behaviors find their power and reason. He is faithful!

> In all my prayers for all of you, I always pray with joy...
> being confident of this, that he who began a good work in
> you will carry it on to completion until the day of Christ
> Jesus (Philippians 1:4,6).

Take a deep breath, my friend. He is faithful and He will complete the work He started in you!

The mirror doesn't lie.

Seeing criticism and cynicism and competition in others is always easier than recognizing or acknowledging it when it shows itself in our mirror. But it is vital that we get honest about this so we can fully engage in this life God has given us as a gift. Do I still find these ugly traits showing up in my mirror? You bet I do. But I am thankful that I don't have to pretend it is not really there. Rather, I can get honest with the God who sees it even better than me, is not surprised or disgusted by this reality, and who stands with me so that we can work on it together.

Personal Response

Critic, Cynic, Competitor, or Cheerleader? Take some time today to do business with your heavenly Father.

What is in your power to do to be at peace with the people who have set themselves up as your critics, cynics, and competitors?

Who needs to be cheered on by you today?

If you are going through this book as a group, take some time to practice cheering each other on according to the other person's bent and personal "path."

> Dear heavenly Father, taking a look in the mirror can be a painful and difficult thing to do. Oftentimes it is so much easier to look through a magnifying glass at the lives of others so that we can avoid the hard work of looking, seeing, and acknowledging the bumps and bruises in our reflection. Give us the strength and the courage to look, really look. Help us to recognize that what we fear we'll see is often, in reality, only about half as bad as what is really there. But help us to also see that this is where Your grace abounds! When our reflection reveals our pain, help us remember that it is Your righteousness we wear and abide in—never our own! Thank You for grace! In Jesus's name, amen.

8

We Are Family!

God has given us gifts to enjoy and to employ.

I have two teenage daughters at the time of this writing. My girls are as different as two girls with shared DNA can be. What's ironic is how different they are from each other and yet how much of myself I can see in each of them. Amelia, my firstborn, is laidback, creative, and very introspective. She wears her heart on her sleeve and tends to get her feelings hurt pretty easily. Macey, the younger of my girls, is more intense, outgoing, and organized. She's more logical than emotional in her outlook on life. She likes things to be a certain way. *Her* way!

These two girls see the world and everything in it through completely different lenses. Not only are they different in personalities and styles, they have the additional challenge of Macey's Asperger's Syndrome and hearing loss to deal with as well. What I've been trying to teach them for the past 16 years is the importance of accepting each other's differences and, in time, appreciating those differences as well. As their mother, I can see the value of these differences. I see what a great team they will be once they have some experience and maturity under their belts, and once they no longer feel the pull to become critics, cynics, and competitors with each other.

Sibling rivalry aside, these girls make one dynamic duo! Where one is weak, the other has strengths. Where one tends to be overly critical of others, the other lends her merciful spirit. Where one is creative, yet disorganized, the one with the administrative gifts can help bring balance. Where one can't stand to see anyone hurting, the other has a strong sense of justice. I see it, and by God's grace I know that one day they will too.

And so it goes within the Body of Christ as a whole. God has gifted all of us differently. We all know that men are from Mars and women are from Venus, but the truth is that not all women are the same as all other women. We bring to each day and each experience all of what we have previously experienced and all that we have inherited genetically to the table. It can be awfully messy at times!

> Each part gets its meaning from the body as a whole, not the other way around (Romans 12:4 MSG).

Before I became a mom, I worked at an apartment community with several other women. I was hired by a higher-up from the corporate office because the property manager had just been promoted and they were in the process of replacing her. From what I had heard from others, the property manager was promoted because she was an exceptional employee. I was really excited about working in such a great environment!

Unfortunately, when the new manager was hired from within the office, the atmosphere changed completely. This woman did not like to work. She did not like to deal with residents. She liked to take three- to four-hour lunches with her friends and hide under her desk (I am not making this up) when she saw a resident walking toward the office from the parking lot. I became pregnant with Amelia while I was an employee there and she would criticize my maternity clothing choices although she wore her husband's wrinkled white undershirts under her suit jacket.

At one point, while she and her friends were off on one of their

endless lunches, the corporate office called. It was the manager who
had been promoted and she asked to speak with the current manager—
who also happened to be her good friend. She called several times that
day, and I could not lie to her. I did not know where the manager was
and I did not know when she would return.

When the former manager had called the third or fourth time, obvi-
ously knowing something fishy was going on, she quit attempting to
reach her friend. Finally, at the end of the day, we were closing up the
apartments we showed potential residents when my boss walked in
laughing and joking with her friends. She went in her office and must
have checked her messages, because when she came out her demeanor
was completely different. She came out to me and the other leasing
agents and let us have it. She screamed at us. She cursed at us. And
she said, "You need to remember something. If you want to move up
in this company, it will only happen because I like you. If I don't like
you, you won't go anywhere, so you need to decide what you're going
to do about that!" If I had not been pregnant and in need of insur-
ance, I would have walked out that day and never walked back in. It
was ridiculous!

How do situations and relationships get that out of control? Why
can't we all just get along? Why do we think life has to be fair—unless
it is unfair in our favor? If the pie slices are of unequal sizes, I won't care
as long as I get the biggest piece!

Rather than operating as a team, our organization was operating
in an "every man for himself" mindset. We could not trust that we
would be treated honorably or that we would be appreciated for the
gifts and talents that we brought to the table. Most likely, it was just a
maturity issue on my manager's part. I have definitely made mistakes
in my youth—good grief, I make mistakes *now!* But how might things
have been different if we had all been able to work with the mindset
that our organization got its meaning from the whole (all of us working together for a common goal) and not the other way around (all of
us working for only one person's benefit)?

Gifted

In Romans 12, as well as other parts of the New Testament, we're told that the Holy Spirit not only gives us Himself at the point of our salvation—which is an amazing reality in and of itself—but that He also gives us gifts to discover, develop, and dispense throughout the rest of our lives.

Read Romans 12:6-8, which shows us the seven motivational gifts given to us by God's Holy Spirit.

> We have different gifts, according to the grace given to each of us. If your gift is prophesying, then prophesy in accordance with your faith; if it is serving, then serve; if it is teaching, then teach; if it is to encourage, then give encouragement; if it is giving, then give generously; if it is to lead, do it diligently; if it is to show mercy, do it cheerfully.

These gifts of the Spirit are given to us at the point of salvation, but are not always discovered right away. It takes time to discover, and then more time to develop, our spiritual gifts.

As you read over these gifts, understand that every believer has at least one of these operating in his or her life, usually more than one, but that no one—other than Jesus Himself—has all of these in full measure. Remember, God created us for relationship, and so the sooner we come to terms with the fact that He wants us to be dependent on others for our individual health and the health of our churches, families, and communities, the better off we'll all be. This means that we need to be diligent to discover our own gifts and then be just as diligent to understand the gifts that others bring to the story that God is writing in our lives.

Discover!

As you read about the motivational gifts of the Spirit, I recommend that you write in the margin the names of those people in your life that you sense have these different gifts.

Prophecy

This is Macey! This person has the keen ability to publicly communicate God's Word in an inspired way that convinces unbelievers and both challenges and comforts believers. They have the ability to persuasively declare God's will. This isn't the same thing as foretelling the future, but "forth-telling" the truth. Prophets tend to see the world as black and white—no gray. They can be very strong-willed and difficult to challenge. When in sync with the Spirit, this gift brings great clarity to the Church as a whole. When operated "in the flesh" (on their own, in their own strength, without allowing the Spirit to flow through them), though, they can be some of the most challenging of people to deal with. John the Baptist and Simon Peter both had this gift.

Service (Ministering/Hospitality)

What would we do without our servants? Nothing would get done! These wonderful people have the ability to see what most of us don't see, and then take the next step of doing something about it. They recognize unmet needs and then go about meeting them. These are the people who bring meals to those who are sick or dealing with a crisis. No one has to remind them or ask them—they just do it. When operating in the Spirit, they can handle it when they don't get a thank-you card, but when operating in the flesh, a lack of gratitude and recognition can be very discouraging and hard to overcome. Biblical examples of people with this gift are Martha and Dorcas.

Teaching

This one always makes me smile because when I took a "Spiritual Gifts Inventory" for the first and second times in my late teens and early twenties, I got my lowest score in this gift. I had no idea what God had planted in the soil of my heart or how He would manifest this gift in me years later. Our words are powerful, and as I dealt unknowingly with people who were critical, cynical, and competitive, I didn't have a clue how their words were impacting me to the point of keeping me quiet.

The teacher has the ability to educate God's people by clearly explaining and applying the Bible in a way that causes them to learn. They have the ability to equip and train other believers for ministry. When operating in the Spirit's power, they are truly a godsend to others as they open up God's Word and their hearts to empower people to go after God's plan for their lives. Within the power of their own abilities, though, they can tend to over-think, over-share, and wear out their welcome by teaching people who don't want a sermon. Biblical examples of people with this gift are Luke and Apollos.

Exhortation

This person has the gift of encouragement. This is my primary motivational gift. Although I do love to teach, my motivation for doing so is to encourage believers to live out of their real identity and to trust God more and more each day. To know that because of Christ in them, they *can* do everything He calls them to do.

Folks with this gift have the ability to motivate God's people to apply and act on biblical principles, especially when they are wavering or discouraged in their faith. They have the ability to bring out the best in others and challenge them to develop their potential. In the Spirit is power, so these are the people you want in your corner. They will give you the encouragement you need to keep on keepin' on. But when they're operating in the flesh (and I know this all too well), they can forget it is Christ who gives them the wisdom to know what to say and when to say it and may miss an opportunity to really engage in what someone's going through by ministering to their heart when they don't need a pep talk, but just a listening ear and soft shoulder. Biblical examples of this type of person are Paul and Barnabas.

Giving

Oh my goodness, what would we do if everyone had the same level of generosity as us? Where would we be without people who have an internal, compelling drive to help fund the work of ministry and other great organizations? God has blessed the Church by gifting some of His children with the ability to earn and manage finances well enough that they are in a position to give generously to worthwhile causes. A giver can't help but give. I don't know where I'd be today if God had not placed givers into my life—people who caught the vision of this ministry to the point that they couldn't help but write a check. When operating in the Spirit, these folks give freely and cheerfully, trusting God to make their investment count. When in the flesh, the tendency is still to give…but not without strings attached. This can get very messy. Biblical examples of people with this gift are Abraham and Zacchaeus.

Administration (Leadership, Ruling)

I am so thankful for people with this gift because I do not have it in full measure! Anyone who has worked with me for very long, or who has paid a visit to my office, knows this is true. I want to be this organized, but it just doesn't come naturally to me. So, because I know how important it is that certain aspects of this ministry are handled in an orderly way, I seek out the help and assistance of those who are able to do this well. Administrators and leaders have the ability to lead and organize people so that organizations are able to perform at full capacity and with the greatest level of effectiveness. In the Spirit is strength, and these people are incredible assets to their families, churches, and workplaces. But as with every gift, watch out if these people start working from their own strength instead. You don't want to cross a leader who operates solely in the flesh. Been there. Done that. It ain't pretty. Biblical examples of this type of person are Nehemiah, Joseph, and Jethro.

Mercy

Ah, the merciful people. They make up a much-needed part of the Body of Christ. I've heard that some people in the Church are full of mercy—but only because they've never shared any of it with anyone! My daughter Amelia has this gift. She will sit with you, listen to your hurts, and offer you a safe place to cry. She genuinely cares about people who are hurting and wants to be the person they can turn to in those times. Mercy's gift also brings with it a great level of discernment. These folks can usually spot a fake a mile away. People with this gift who allow the Spirit to flow through them bring healing to the hearts of others and peace to situations in chaos. When operating in the flesh, though, they can be thin-skinned and overly judgmental of people whenever they don't see them as being "real." Biblical examples of people with this gift are John and Ruth.

Where do you see yourself in these gifts? Have you discovered your motivational gift? If so, how are you currently using it?

Develop!

Once we discover how God has gifted us, it becomes our responsibility to get actively involved in the development of those gifts. God is the giver of the gift and He is also the one who brings the gifts to maturity—but He will not do this without our trust and cooperation. Remember, He is a relational being. He invites us to participate with Him in this, but will never, ever force this on any of us. We serve a God who is a gentleman.

Discovering our gifts can take more time than we like, but is totally worth the effort and pain—and sometimes embarrassment—it takes to get there. Developing these gifts takes a lifetime. We aren't going to get this perfectly right, and that's okay! God knows we're human and He knows we're going to mess things up from time to time, and He is not swayed by this in the least.

When I was younger, I was desperate to find God's will for my life and learn how He wanted to use me in my generation. I took all the tests that were supposed to reveal how God had gifted me, but as far as I could tell, He hadn't. I remember really struggling with this—wanting to know my purpose and how I could make a real difference.

When I was in my early twenties, I shared this angst with a woman who was ten or fifteen years older than me. Although I know she was trying to help, it only made me feel worse when she said, "Shelley,

God has gifted you to be a good friend. Everyone needs a good friend."
What? I felt so patronized. I know she meant well. She just wanted to
make me feel better. But my desire was to know that I had something
unique to offer in this life. I didn't want to be what anyone could be; I
wanted to be what God had designed *me* to be. I just didn't have a clue
who or what that was.

It took a long time, and a lot of mistakes, but God used each experience to help me discover and then begin to develop the gifts He had
given me. I began to pay attention to those things that energized me
rather than depleted me. I began to recognize what most irked me in
others—like when someone would use their words to tear someone
down or belittle someone rather than encourage them. Little by little,
God began unveiling the gifts He had placed in me and then lovingly
invited me into opportunities whereby these gifts could be developed
and used.

Develop your gifts by using them! Allow yourself to make some
mistakes along the way—God will use even those! I served God in a
lot of different ways before coming to understand my own gifts and
how and where to use them. I sang in the choir. I taught elementary
Sunday School classes. (It didn't take long for me to realize this was *not*
my gift!) I helped organize events at the church for women's ministry. I
worked in the counseling department and assisted the financial counselor. I served as a secretary in different classes, helping keep the meeting organized. I sent cards each week to people who had not been in
church the Sunday before.

I did a lot of things before I ever felt clear on what God put me
here to do. And you know what? He has used each and every bit of that
experience to increase my effectiveness in what I do today. It all mattered. It all counted. None of it was wasted time. So if you want to discover your gifts, or if you are at the place where you want to develop
them so that you will be ready when God says "Let's go—it's time,"
then just start somewhere. Do something. He'll clarify your path in His
perfect timing. But if you wait until you feel the time is perfect, you
will never leave the starting line.

Dispense!

As we learn to humbly appreciate our own gifts and who God has made us to be, we begin to enjoy the freedom we experience. This freedom enables us to allow and enjoy who God made other people to be as well. As we share our gifts with others in practical and Spirit-led ways, we increase the health of the Body of Christ.

We're created to be interdependent and not independent. Want to learn the secret of going further faster? Start by dispensing your God-given gifts in an environment where others are empowered to do the same.

Discover!
Develop!
Dispense!

Vive la Différence!

We've looked together at the variety of ways God has made us all so unique from one another. Not only has God given us different spiritual gifts, but He's also given us different personality types. Added to the fact that we all have different experiences, backgrounds, cultural preferences, and DNA, understanding differences in personalities can go a long way toward helping us do our part to be at peace with everyone…even when others are not doing their part to be at peace with us. Looking at a situation through another person's perspective can be very helpful, can't it? Just as I would love to be able to program my kids to do this with one another, because I know they'd appreciate one another so much more, God

> Knowing that we're all different isn't the same thing as accepting these differences. And accepting them isn't the same thing as appreciating them.

wants us to begin to see that the gifts He imparted to us, different as they are, are really wonderful things!

I used to try so hard to be the kind of woman I thought God wanted me to be. I thought He wanted me to be a quiet, good-at-everything-domestic wife and mom. I tried very hard to be that woman and felt very inadequate around the women for whom this came easily. I believed for a long time that in order for me to be acceptable, I had to be perfect. This will exhaust the best of us.

I tried to operate in the gift of mercy (I guess I thought it was the most feminine and spiritual of the seven gifts), but often felt drained by the output of that energy. You know why? Because I was bringing my *own* energy and power to each of these circumstances. As I began to learn how God made *me* and began to use those gifts He gave me on purpose, everything began to change; and one of the biggest changes was in how much I could enjoy being around the women I had previously tried to emulate. Now I could celebrate them instead.

Whose power source are you plugging into?

When God first called me to ministry, one of the first people I spoke to about the calling was a pastor named Jim Law. Jim is very wise and also very funny, so when he speaks I know I'm about to become wiser or get a good laugh. Either way it's a win, so I listen intently.

Jim said something back in 2004 that has never left me. He said, "Shelley, what God initiates, God will sustain. So if God has called you, then He will sustain you—He'll give you the resources, the finances, the energy, and the wisdom to perform that which He has called you to do. But the opposite holds true as well: What man initiates, man must sustain. So if you get outside of the Spirit's leadership, and you begin to pursue even good things in your own energy, then the pressure to sustain it rests on you alone." He had my attention. I definitely want to allow the Spirit to fully operate with His power in my life. It scares me to death to think of how things will go if I forget this principle and I try to make things happen—even things I'm gifted for—in my own power.

Remember that these seven motivating forces are *gifts!* Don't treat them like they are anything less. Don't allow yourself to see them as crosses you must bear just because you may find it challenging to accept how someone else views a situation or handles a responsibility. When someone sees or perceives or feels differently than you, realize it just might be the lens through which she views life. What could happen if we all decided to give grace to other people for where they are on their walk with the Lord? We're all at different places of maturity and we've all had different experiences. What if we began to take this into consideration more often? Maybe this would be one step toward doing all we can to be at peace with everyone as we live out of our new nature and the godly identity we have now through Christ.

Did you happen to notice that my daughters have polar opposite gifts? You can't get much different than a Prophet and a person with Mercy as their motivation in life! But as they grow in the nurture and admonition of their Lord, they will begin to see how incredible this is. It may be difficult on them—and on me!—at times in this season in our lives, but as they've already done some growing and maturing, I'm receiving a blessing. I've watched God begin to reveal how beautifully gifted they both are and how much more effective they are when they work together rather than against each other.

As members of the Body of Christ, when we begin to live in unity and love, remembering who we are, walking in the Spirit of humility with one another, we become a powerful force for God and for good in our culture, family, workplace, neighborhoods, and churches.

As my pastor, Andy Stanley, says, "Rather than becoming a critic, become a student."

Personal Response

Why do you suppose God often puts us in situations and relationships with people who are gifted so differently from us, even though He knows this will be challenging for those involved?

Consider Jim Law's advice to me back in 2004. How can this advice help you to discover, develop, and dispense your motivational gifts of the Spirit?

Dear heavenly Father, Your graciousness knows no bounds! Thank You for how You have given each of us amazing gifts that build up the Body of Christ when empowered by the Holy Spirit in us. Help us to acknowledge and affirm these gifts in others—and in ourselves! Give us joy in using them often and in creative ways. Let the truth of Your love and favor motivate us to action with an attitude of celebration! In Jesus's name, amen.

Check out more from Shelley at
www.shelleyhendrix.org/2012/02
/gods-plans-are-so-much-better-than-mine.html

9

Live *Your* Life

*If it is possible, as far as it depends on
you, live at peace with everyone.*

ROMANS 12:18

So far we've looked at the first two of six principles that we can, through Christ who strengthens us, put into practice in our lives in order to do our part to be at peace with everyone.

> I can do all this through him who gives me strength (Philippians 4:13).

You've probably noticed by now that I'm not giving you six easy steps to be everyone's BFF by Friday. Anyone who promises you an easy way to make hard changes in your life is not someone to be believed! God never promised quick and easy solutions to any challenge we face in life. But what He does promise is far better. He promises us His grace to make it through anything and everything that comes our way and He offers us some practical principles that, when implemented into our lives over time, begin to make a big and lasting difference.

Sufficient Grace

> But he said to me, "My grace is sufficient for you, for my
> power is made perfect in weakness." Therefore I will boast
> all the more gladly about my weaknesses, so that Christ's
> power may rest on me (2 Corinthians 12:9).

Take your physical health for example. Any real and lasting change that is going to be good for you is going to take a decision made in the present, followed by actions taken presently and moving forward. It is so easy to commit your future self to something your present self should already have been doing in the past. How many times have we said on Sunday that the diet and exercise would begin on Monday? It is so easy to commit our future self to good things, isn't it?

As we take a look at these principles together, realize that God is indeed going to empower you by His grace to do the things He is calling you to do, because it *is* His Spirit in you after all, but He isn't going to make you put any of these principles into place.

Let's quickly review what we've covered so far:

Principle 1: Offer yourself as a living sacrifice by being intentional with God's Word and by willingly humbling yourself before God and others.

Principle 2: Accept and appreciate the differences you see in others.

Principle 3: Live Out of Who God Says You Are

> Let love be without hypocrisy. Abhor what is evil; cling
> to what is good. Be devoted to one another with broth-
> erly love, give preference to one another in honor; not
> lagging behind in diligence, fervent in spirit, serving the
> Lord; rejoicing in hope, persevering in tribulation, devoted
> to prayer; contributing to the needs of the saints, practicing
> hospitality. Bless those who persecute you; bless and do not
> curse. Rejoice with those who rejoice, and weep with those
> who weep (Romans 12:9-15 NASB).

Quite the to-do list, huh? Just trying to do all of these in one day would exhaust me. Brush teeth. Take out the trash. Do the dishes. Love well. Give generously. Cry with people who are crying. Pray a lot. Do the laundry. Feed the family. Be nice to mean people. And this is on top of being a living sacrifice and accepting and appreciating the differences in others...Is this something we're seriously expected, nay *required*, to do?

Let's take another look at this passage, this time in the words of the Message:

> Love from the center of who you are; don't fake it. Run for dear life from evil; hold on for dear life to good. Be good friends who love deeply; practice playing second fiddle. Don't burn out; keep yourselves fueled and aflame. Be alert servants of the Master, cheerfully expectant. Don't quit in hard times; pray all the harder. Help needy Christians; be inventive in hospitality. Bless your enemies; no cursing under your breath. Laugh with your happy friends when they're happy; share tears when they're down.

Live *your* life—the one God gave you!

It comes down to this: loving from the center of who you are. My understanding of who I am is the second most important thing about me. A.W. Tozer taught that what comes to mind when we think about God is the most important thing about us. [5] I agree. An accurate concept of God will lead me to an accurate concept of myself—and others.

Knowing God takes time and commitment to the relationship. When I was younger, I envied the depth of intimacy I saw that a few people had with their Creator. I would hear these rare ones pray and my heart would flip-flop inside me. On the one hand, their relationship with God gave me such hope that perhaps one day I could experience this as well. On the other, an intimate relationship with God seemed hopeless and unattainable for someone like me.

When you think of God, what comes into your mind first? (Be as honest as you can be, even if the answer isn't something you'd want others to know just yet.)

For so long, I saw God as a distant, all-powerful, unemotional judge. He didn't have a face that I could picture. He was just far away and yet watching every little move I made. Without realizing it, I made this internal vow that one day, and in some way, I'd get things right with Him so He and I could finally be close. I didn't know it back then, but this drive to finally please Him was the motivating force behind all of my ministry efforts and my striving to do good works.

I didn't know then how many other people could identify with this same motivation. We tend to either be people who try really hard or people who don't see the value in putting forth the effort. I was a *try hard* person. My husband, Stephen, was the type who didn't see the value in putting forth the effort. I was convinced that if I tried hard enough, one day I'd get it right. I refused to give up. Stephen, on the other hand, didn't see the point in trying because he knew he'd never measure up anyway. We were both afraid of the same thing: rejection. And we were both longing for the same thing: unconditional love and acceptance. We just didn't know we already had it.

When I was married the first time, I tried really hard to do things for my husband that I knew he would appreciate. I cooked his favorite meals often. I made sure he had clean clothes for work. I tried to keep myself in good shape and take good care of the kids and the house. I did my best to work within our meager budget and be available to him as his best friend. He still left.

I'm married again, and have been for over a decade. I do all of those same things for Stephen as I did before. You know what the difference is? My motive.

I was trying really hard in my first marriage to prove my love to my husband so that one day, he'd see this and it would move him to love me again. To be proud that I was his. With Stephen, I do these things but for a completely different reason: I do it because I am loved so well. I do these things because I know I'm loved and cared for and that he's proud I'm his wife. Knowing I am loved is a far stronger and more compelling reason to offer my best and take those risks in relationship than fear ever was!

But this change in motive isn't only a result of knowing Stephen loves me. I've come to see that this same thing has happened in my relationship with my heavenly Father. For so long, I obeyed and tried to do the right thing in hopes that those things would finally add up to a big enough pile of gifts that would make Him reachable. If I could stack the bricks high enough, I'd be able to climb the tower to where He was and He would see how much I loved Him—and maybe, just maybe, He'd be proud I was His child. As proud of me as He seemed to be of others.

I know I'm not alone. We pretend this kind of thing isn't true about us because it is hardly impressive. But you know what? I got really tired of trying to be impressive. (Besides, no one ever seemed all that impressed anyways.) Pastor Joel Hunter once said, "We respect strength, but we connect at weakness."[6] The trouble with trying to impress people is that it not only erects a wall between us (due to that whole comparison thing), but it sets me up for failure. I've placed myself in a position where I have to be impressive every time I'm with that person in order to maintain her impression of me. And that is exhausting!

When I connect with someone, it frees me up to be the real me in every interaction—on good days as well as the bad. I stop being the star of my life and I can point people to the One who is. I'd much rather connect with someone than impress them any day. This is living out of who God says I am. This is learning to love from the center of *who I am*.

Do you strive to impress with your strengths or connect at weakness? How so?

In Romans 12:9-15, we're given several ways that we can choose to do our part in living in peace with others. But if we don't get the "center of who we are" part right, this list will become a chain around our ankles, causing us to stumble, when it's meant to be a banner over us, describing all that we are capable of doing.

"Love must be sincere," Paul says in Romans 12:9. Our love will have the power to be the real thing when we begin to believe that God really is who He says He is and that He will do what He says He will do. It begins to be the real thing when we begin to trust that we are who He says we are as well. It begins when we learn to love from the center of ourselves.

I've heard Joyce Meyer say on many occasions that if you need to take a year and do nothing but learn what it means to be "in Christ," you should do it. You will not ever regret it. We have an enemy who will use everything in his arsenal to keep the believer from knowing who she is in Christ and what is available to her. Don't let him win this all-important battle with you. He can't rob you of your identity, but he'll do his best to keep you from ever finding out what it is.

> Therefore, if anyone is in Christ, the new creation has come;
> The old has gone, the new is here (2 Corinthians 5:17)!

As I begin to understand that I am a brand new creation—not an improved version of who I was, but something altogether new—and as I begin to live out of who God says I am, I begin to behave in a completely different way as I submit in trust to the process of growth and maturity. I can begin to celebrate the times when I find myself trust-ing God more rather than keeping score of how well I measure up on the "sin-o-meter."

Second Corinthians 5:17 reveals that we become brand new cre-ations at the point of our salvation. This is nothing short of a miracle. The old is gone, and the new has come. The old has *died*. You know what it means when someone dies. They can no longer get up, move around, or talk to us. They no longer have the power to do so. They pass away, but their influence remains.

Take my mother-in-law, for example. Jackie Hendrix welcomed me into her home and family in the warmest way. I cannot remember one time when I didn't know that she loved and accepted me. She wel-comed my girls into her family as though they were her own grandchil-dren. Jackie wasn't perfect, but she got closer to the bar than most of us!

Jackie got very sick and after a long, arduous battle, she passed away. She slipped into eternity to be with her Savior. She has perished, but you know what remains? Her influence. My memories of her are still very vivid. She had a lot of funny sayings, and they still crack my hus-band and me up when we reminisce about his mom. There are a bunch of "Jackie-isms" that keep her memory close to us. We loved her so much we named our only son, Jackson, after her. She was one of a kind.

Jackie's father passed away long before I ever came into the Hendrix family. He had his own struggles in life and was never exactly a model husband or father. Jackie endured a great deal of hardship because of his abusive behavior. Although he had passed away many years before I ever met her, his influence remained in her life and continued to influ-ence her greatly.

You see, just because someone passes away and loses their "power" doesn't mean the power of their influence passes away with them. So it goes with our old nature—or our old way of life, of thinking, of feel-ing or believing. This takes time and grace to overcome. The old has passed away, but it still lingers in our memories and attitudes, doesn't it? We need to recognize this in our own lives and in the lives of others if we're going to experience peace by learning to live out of who God says we are. Now. Today. Because of Christ in us!

The old has passed away. What does this mean to you?

The new has come. How is this cause for celebration?

The influence remains. How should this reality affect the way we view our identity and our struggle to trust God's love for us?

How can this understanding help us to forgive others who have hurt us? (After all, they are dealing with the influence of their old nature too.)

Love from the Center of Who You Are

Sometimes I love others because it is easy to do. On most days, it is very easy for me to love my husband and my children. *Most days*. But even on most days, there are people that I interact with or encounter who are definitely not easy to love. And truth be told, I'm not always easy to love either. What are we supposed to do in those situations?

> Be devoted to one another in love. Honor one another
> above yourselves (Romans 12:10).

In my home, there are times when my kids just cannot see eye-to-eye with one another and reach an impasse. I can't count the number of times I've said to them, "Do you love *me*?" (I'm fortunate that they always say yes.) And they've since learned what comes next: "Then, because of your love for me, and knowing how much I love each of you, will you please show love to one another out of respect to me?" This is *phileo* love—brotherly love. And God calls us to love others like this.

I think this is what God whispers to us when it comes to our conflicts with other members in our family of faith. *Do you love me? Do you trust that I love you? Do you believe I love her too? Then will you show her love for my sake?* We share the same name: Jesus. Shouldn't that be reason enough to show love—unconditional love—to one another? I feel convicted each and every time I think about this. I remember the person I allowed myself to judge because I felt jealous that she was blessed in a way I haven't been. I remember the times I've allowed myself to be bitter toward someone who wronged me instead of offering her grace, knowing that if she recognized her own value and worth she would never have intentionally wounded me.

God calls us to this kind of love and also equips us to love in this way. Just another amazing miracle designed and delivered by our incredible heavenly Father!

"We share the same name. Shouldn't that be reason enough to show love to one another?" How does this statement sit with you?

This principle of loving from the center of who we are by living out of who God says we are isn't something we need to put pressure on ourselves to master overnight—or even in this lifetime. We are human beings, after all. We will not get this right every time, but as we apply the truths of God's Word to our lives more and more, we'll see the fruit of the Spirit showing up in our lives. The seeds of the fruit already dwell within the soil of the heart that has trusted Christ, and in the perfect timing, as those seeds are nurtured, we will *grow!*

A few years ago I was struggling to make a big decision. This wasn't a decision about what I was going to make for dinner or what color shirt I'd wear the next day; this was a decision with long-term impact. I don't mean to be overly dramatic, but I was in some serious turmoil over what to do. I sought the counsel of a wise friend and told her how I could handle whatever the consequences would be if I only knew that in the end, I had done the right thing. I asked her what she thought I should do…and you know what? She didn't give me advice one way or the other. She simply asked, "Shelley, is your Jesus too small and too weak to redeem a mistake you might make?"

During another difficult decision-making season in my life, I sought the counsel of another wise woman who said, "Your life is in His will, Shelley, so you are free to make your decision and trust God with the path you are on." This isn't to say that our decisions and choices don't matter, but it is sad how crippled we can become out of fear that God's love isn't big enough to redeem a mistake we might make or a mistake we've already made.

Take a few minutes to prayerfully and slowly read the lines of this hymn written by Frederick Martin Lehman:

> The love of God is greater far
> than tongue or pen can ever tell.
> It goes beyond the highest star
> and reaches to the lowest hell.
> The guilty pair, bowed down with care,
> God gave His son to win;
> His erring child He reconciled
> and pardoned from his sin.
>
> O love of God, how rich and pure!
> How measureless and strong!

It shall forevermore endure
the saints' and angels' song.

When years of time shall pass away,
and earthly thrones and kingdoms fall,
When men who here refuse to pray,
on rocks and hills and mountains call;
God's love, so sure, shall still endure,
all measureless and strong;
Redeeming grace to Adam's race—
the saints' and angels' song.

Could we with ink the ocean fill,
and were the skies of parchment made,
were every stalk on earth a quill,
and every man a scribe by trade;
to write the love of God above
would drain the ocean dry;
nor could the scroll contain the whole,
though stretched from sky to sky.

Personal Response

You are loved deeply by the One who created you. Take a few minutes to read over the following passages and jot down what this reveals about how your heavenly Father feels about YOU.

> Because of his great love for us, God, who is rich in mercy, made us alive with Christ even when we were dead in transgressions—it is by grace you have been saved. And God raised us up with Christ and seated us with him in the heavenly realms in Christ Jesus (Ephesians 2:4-6).

> I have loved you with an everlasting love; I have drawn you with unfailing kindness. I will build you up again (Jeremiah 31:3-4).

> For I am convinced that neither death nor life, neither angels nor demons, neither the present nor the future, nor

any powers, neither height nor depth, nor anything else in all creation, will be able to separate us from the love of God that is in Christ Jesus our Lord (Romans 8:38-39).

Fyodor Dostoyevsky once wrote that "To truly love someone is to see them as God intended." What do you think he meant by that?

Based on the reading you've done today and what God is showing you through Scripture, what does God see when He looks at you?

Based on this, what does God see when He looks at the person who has wounded you?

Oh, heavenly Father, that we might begin to grasp the unsearchable depths of Your amazing love for us! That would change everything! Remove the barriers that keep us from trusting Your love and as You do, remove the blinders that cause us to miss the beauty You desire us to see in Your other children. Help us to trust You as You continue to work on our hearts and minds. In Jesus's name, amen.

Part Three

Put Your Big-Girl Pants On and Deal with It!

I have a dear friend who says this quite often when under stress. As women, we seem to have a higher stress tolerance than our male counterparts. We can be sick as dogs and still somehow manage to get our mile-long to-do lists completed, can't we? While it's admirable to be able to "just deal with it," we need to be cautious about how we do this. In this next section, we'll talk about *maturity* and look for ways to be intentional, cooperating with God as He works in our lives to take us all on to a higher level of living with Him. Yes, even in those really, really challenging relationships!

10

I Get By with a Little Help from My Friends

It is the friends you can call up at 4 a.m. that matter.
MARLENE DIETRICH

There are so many lessons I want to teach my daughters from my own experiences. Lessons that took far too long and cost me far too much pain to learn. Can you relate? It took me until my late twenties to finally internalize one of the most important lessons I would ever learn. (I'm so grateful for God's patience with me!) Although it took me a while to get this, I am eternally grateful that I did (eventually) get it. You know those mile-marking, game-changing, life-altering lessons you learn that mold you into the person you are today? Well, this was one of those for me.

Because I was a pastor's daughter, I was known in just about every circle I entered. I was a medium-sized fish in a very tiny little puddle of a pond, but I didn't know that. All I knew was that wherever I went, people seemed to know who I was. That made me feel pretty secure and somewhat significant. Again, I didn't know any *different*, so I didn't know any *better*. This lasted all the way through fifth grade. (Which seemed like an entire lifetime back then!)

Then, between fifth and sixth grades everything changed. My dad was no longer a pastor and we were no longer attending church. Without realizing what I was doing, I began my quest to find that security and significance in other ways. I didn't know what the pull was or why it was so strong, but I tried and tried to become friends with all the "right" people, especially when I began attending church on my own again once I was in high school. The first church I attended on my own embraced me with open arms. It was one of the best experiences of my life. It wasn't perfect by any means, and I definitely got hurt by some folks during those two years or so, but overall, God used it to get His girl back up close to Him—and for that, I will always be so grateful.

But all was not well at home. My parents' marriage had deteriorated to the point of divorce and just before my sixteenth birthday, I had to decide which parent to live with. It was one of the most painful decisions I ever had to make. So painful that I decided I couldn't make it. I let my little sister decide and my choice was to go with whomever she went with. It meant that I could look out for her…and that I wouldn't have to feel responsible for rejecting one of my parents. It was a no-win situation all around.

I made a deal with God. I told Him that if He got either one of my parents into a good church, I would live with that parent. It didn't matter what church or where. I just knew that if either of them went, I'd leave the one I was attending and I'd go with them.

When my mom filed for divorce, my dad returned to church. It wasn't long after that I remembered my promise and kept it. The church was much larger than the one I'd been attending and I was intimidated at first. I didn't want to start all over making new friends, but I had promised God, right? This church ended up being a great one and a big part of my life. It was the church where I grew in my walk with God more than any other. It is the church where I was called to ministry. It is the church where I dedicated my babies and married my husband. It is one of the greatest places on earth.

But there is no such place as perfect this side of heaven. Try as I might, I couldn't become friends with some of the girls (and later the women) that I wanted to be friends with. It was as though there was a door in between me and these women, and for whatever reason, I was always left standing on the outside of that door. (Sound familiar?) It seemed that they could be friends with just about anyone—except me. I came to this church with no label. I wasn't impressive by any stretch of the imagination. I was basically invisible. Don't get me wrong—I had and still have some amazing friends there, but it was the handful of females I tried to be friends with and who gave me the cold shoulder over and over again whom God used to teach me one of the best—and yet most painful—lessons of my life.

Describe an experience where you too felt as though you were on the "outside of the door."

Being the new kid can be so hard (in a school, a workplace, a church, or a family). Have you ever experienced this? Was your experience positive or negative, and how so?

Live in harmony with one another. Do not be proud, but be willing to associate with people of low position. Do not be conceited (Romans 12:16).

I finally got sick and tired of wondering what was wrong with me. They weren't "mean girls," but they were ice cold. They would only be friendly to me or acknowledge me if I approached them first or if there was another person present whom, I can only assume, they wanted to impress. Otherwise I was invisible and ignored. It was one thing to experience this in a secular environment, but at church? And at one I had been a part of for so long? It felt like a game where everyone knew the rules except for me. And whether they wanted to keep playing or not, I didn't care. I was tired of it.

Why do you think females especially play these kinds of games?

Even with those kinds of relational hurts in my story, I'm actually thankful for those experiences. Now, if you had told me this would be the case back then, I probably couldn't have imagined it. *But then God…*

At one point in this journey, my daughter Macey was hospitalized. She was only eight months old and I was a young mommy scared to death. During that week-long stay in the hospital not one person from my church stopped by or even called to see how we were doing. I was crushed. I had decided that perhaps that particular church had outgrown me and my little family.

Over the course of the next couple of years, God really worked in my heart. For one, as I allowed my hurt to turn to resentment and began visiting other churches, God asked me a question. "Shelley, when was the last time you visited someone in the hospital or let someone know that you missed them in church?" This was not the voice of condemnation. This was the gentle, convicting voice of the Holy Spirit. And He got through to me loud and clear. I realized that if I left that body of believers for the wrong reason, I would live to regret it. I knew I would eventually miss out on something valuable God had for me. I asked God to show me how to be more intentional to reach out to others instead of always hoping and waiting for them to reach out to me.

I had to let go of the bitterness left from the painful wounds. I had to forget about the baby shower my Bible study class hadn't thrown me during my first pregnancy when they threw one for the two women who were due at the same time I was. I had to let go of the fact that I wasn't included in all the girls' outings and trips. I had to place rejection after rejection into my heavenly Father's hands and entrust my life and my journey to Him.

The second big "Aha!" moment for me was several years later. I was battling the tug of war in my heart between the desires to allow God to use me in the lives of others and desperately wanting to feel affirmed by the "right" people. I remember it clearly, like it was yesterday. I was in my car, mulling all of this over and wondering why I experienced so much rejection from other women. What was wrong with me? And out of nowhere, to my spirit, God said, "Shelley, why do you keep trying to be friends with people who already seem to have enough friends? Why don't you begin looking for those who feel the same way you do—invisible—and become their friend?" And you know what? I decided to try that approach, since the one I had been employing for so long wasn't working out so well. This one alteration in my life changed me completely. Once I took my focus off the faces of those who had rejected me time and again, once I stopped trying to figure out *why*, I was free. Free to be a friend to someone who wanted my friendship.

> The only way to have a friend is to be one.
>
> —Ralph Waldo Emerson

Do you know of someone who may be looking for your friendship? If so, who is she?

Are you interested in forming a friendship with her?

If not, why not?

If so, what is stopping you?

I began to look for those women who were new to my church and new to my area. I found that since I had been there for so long, I knew a lot of different people and could "matchmake" friends pretty easily. I knew all the best stores and shortcuts in our area, so I shared those with people who were unfamiliar with the town. I made the best friends of my life—but it took God removing the blinders from my eyes, showing me all of these amazing women who were right there all along.

The Message translates Romans 12:16 this way: "Get along with each other; don't be stuck-up. Make friends with nobodies; don't be the great somebody."

Principle 4: Choose Your Friends Wisely

We tell our kids to choose their friends wisely, don't we? And for good reason too. We've been around the bend enough times to know how influential people can be, especially when we spend time with them on a regular basis. I've shared with you how difficult some relationships with other women have been for me, and I know you have your own war stories as well. But before we give up completely, let's keep walking this path, one step at a time.

My mom gave me some really good advice when I was a teenager. It was a time when some friends of mine began making decisions that would take them down the wrong path. She said, "You can be *friendly* to just about anyone, but this doesn't mean you have to be *friends* with everyone." Good advice, don't you think?

My mom gave me a valuable gift when she told me this. I realized that I don't have to take on all the world's issues or try to fix anyone. I also don't have to try continuously to become friends with someone who has shown no interest in a friendship with me.

I've heard it said that ten percent of people are just not going to like you. There is nothing you can do about this. You can free yourself quite a bit when you allow yourself to be okay with this and simply give yourself permission to be unliked by a few people. I can simply be who God made me to be and allow His Spirit to flow through my life and into the lives of others as He sees fit. There will be those people who I can bring into my inner circle, and there will be those who need to stay out of that circle…at least for a while. Spending time practicing Principle 1 helps me to make the distinction between the two.

What is Principle 1?

Explain the difference between being friends with someone and being friendly to someone. Why is this an important distinction to make when it comes to being at peace with everyone?

We've already established that God designed us for relationship and that He designed women uniquely in that we *need* relationships—close relationships—with other females for our health. Remember Anne Shirley and her "bosom friend" Diana Barry in the Anne of Green Gables books? Whether we'll admit it or not, depending on how we've been influenced by relationships in the past, we all want this kind of kindred friendship. We want someone who knows us completely, faults and all, and yet loves us all the more for knowing everything there is to know about us.

Do you have a friend like this? If so, what makes her and your friendship so special to you?

Women need one another. So why are we so hard on each other? Why so suspicious? We tend to compare our lives and every little detail of them with every little detail we can see in others. "Am I heavier than she is?" "She is so pretty. I wonder if she's had any *work* done on her." "Her house is so much nicer than mine." "I wish my husband wrote those kinds of messages to me on my Facebook wall." "I wish I had an 'honor roll student' sticker to put on my car!"

And when we compare, we tend to put that other woman up on a pedestal above us, or we put her down as though she is beneath us. "If she'd just try a little harder or put more effort into it, she could be thinner/happier/more spiritual too…" "What kind of mother allows her children to do *that?*" It is offensive to us as we read this, and it is heartbreaking to the Father who loves us all as equals.

Comparing Leads to Competition Leads to Conflict

When it all comes down to it, we have far more that unites us than divides us. Unfortunately, we often allow those superficial differences to keep us from becoming friends with people who aren't just like us. I had a friend who had to quit a job he loved because the people he worked with were mostly of one denomination and he was of a different one. They all claimed Jesus as Lord and Savior of their lives, and yet the coworkers continued to harass my friend to try to get him "converted" to their denomination. It became so difficult for him to perform his duties on the job that he ended up leaving that company—and it was truly their loss.

We must come to the realization that as sisters in Christ, we all get to be our Daddy's favorite! He isn't looking at the labels we often ascribe to ourselves or others, and He doesn't give any thought to the labels people place on us. He just loves us. Just as we are.

> Go through your phone book, call people, and ask them to drive you to the airport. The ones who will drive you are your true friends. The rest aren't bad people—they're just acquaintances.
>
> —Jay Leno

I had a dear friend who passed away not too long ago. Her name was Lyla. She was so fun to be around. I loved having time to spend with her and it wasn't until she was close to death after a battle with cancer that I fully understood why. Lyla was so loved by so many in part because each and every one of us felt like we were her favorite. Oh, how I want that to be true of me! I'm a long way away from that goal, but I've seen the example of it, and I desire it to be something people sense when they're with me. It is one of the best things about God: He loves us all as though we were His absolute favorite, and this takes nothing away from any of us.

Have you ever known a person like Lyla? Describe this person and how you felt in his or her presence.

Choose your friends wisely…

Do you know why I think God handpicked me out of the many far more qualified people to be the one who would obey His call to begin a ministry like Church 4 Chicks? I know it is not because I'm the brightest bulb in the box—because I'm not. It is not because I have any impressive labels—I've already told you I was the "invisible woman" for most of my life. It is not because I brought influence or financial prosperity or even an engaging personality to the table—because I didn't. I honestly believe He called me to do this because He had allowed me to experience enough rejection, abandonment, and downright meanness both within and without the walls of the church. He knew I would have compassion for other women who had experienced the same hurt, and by His grace He gave me an opportunity to join Him in doing something to fix the problem.

Most of us *chicks* in the church have heard Titus 2:3-5. It is our "go-to" verse on female relationships:

> Likewise, teach the older women to be reverent in the way they live, not to be slanderers or addicted to much wine, but to teach what is good. Then they can urge the younger women to love their husbands and children, to be self-controlled and pure, to be busy at home, to be kind, and to be subject to their husbands, so that no one will malign the word of God.

> Be courteous with all, but intimate with a few, and let those few be well tried before you give them your confidence. True friendship is a plant of slow growth, and must undergo and withstand the shocks of adversity before it is entitled to the appellation.
>
> —George Washington

When we as women choose to come together in real, authentic, and honest relationships with one another, we all win. Rather than clinging to our own agenda and ideas of what our "friend list" should look like, we open ourselves up to the possibilities of all God has in store for us in our relationships.

Take me for example. I've always had some pretty good and even great friendships with a few key people—and that's great. But I'm so thankful that God allowed me to feel the sting of rejection from those who didn't want to be my friends. This put me in a position to receive the gift of friendship with women He has sovereignly placed in my life—women I never would have expected. Several come to my mind right now and all I can do is smile and thank God for knowing me and loving me enough to give me what was best rather than what I asked Him for.

Personal Response

How would you describe the most important friendships you've had in your life?

Have you ever "jumped the gun" in friendship rather than waiting on God's timing for the relationship to develop? Describe that experience and what you learned from it.

In Romans 12, we're taught to choose our close friends wisely and associate with the humble. So often we allow ourselves to get caught up trying to initiate friendships with people who are just like us or who can possibly promote us in some way (through their social status, career, ministry, etc.) rather than choosing friends who would be good for our souls and whom we could bless in return. Taking an honest look in the mirror, where are you spending most of your energy when it comes to developing friendships?

Many of our "peace-robbing" issues come from the fact that we allow ourselves to be mistreated by people we have no business associating with in the first place. Do you agree or disagree with this statement?

Let's face facts: Some women just don't like to form friendships with other women. It isn't hard to find women who will tell you that their best friends are guys. Why do you think this happens?

Dear heavenly Father, we recognize that relationships are extremely significant. Help us to choose our closest friends wisely. Help us to hear Your voice as You guide us into the relationships You have for us. Help us to be content if our offer of friendship is rejected. May we never put any friendship with another person above our friendship with You. In Jesus's name, amen.

11

Off the Hook

Forgiveness is the fragrance that the violet sheds
on the heel that has crushed it.
MARK TWAIN

The man I've called "Pastor" most of my life has said, more times than I can count, that sometimes he has felt "as nervous as a long-tailed cat in a room full of rocking chairs!" That's exactly how I would describe my first experiences with public speaking. Oh my goodness. I would feel completely and utterly sick to my stomach. I made so many trips to the restroom and would sometimes feel like I was going to faint. I still get nervous at times, but nothing like I did in those first years of ministry.

One thing that always helped calm my nerves was seeing friendly faces looking back at me. It helped a lot to know I was connecting with the people listening! But from time to time, I would notice someone who looked downright mad. I would do two things at once when this happened. I'd continue talking, but my brain was also having a conversation with itself. It went something like this: "I wonder what I said that made her so mad." *"Maybe she isn't mad. Maybe she just isn't listening."* "I don't know what's worse." "*Maybe she just doesn't like you.*" "That doesn't help." "*Maybe she is taking notes to give to the pastor who is going to call you to the office to handle the complaint and then you will never get to teach again.*" "What was I just saying?"

I can name at least four different instances where this occurred. And I can also tell you that in all of those times, the very woman I was looking at and fretting about came up to tell me how much she got out of what I shared and how God used it in her life. A few of them are my close friends today. We are so crazy sometimes, aren't we?

It Doesn't Take Much

A *perceived* threat. Sometimes that is all it takes for unpleasant friction to show itself in our relationships. That is what was happening to me in these situations. I thought I was being judged unfairly. I perceived something. Not a threat necessarily, but a *perceived* threat. And because we all have different experiences, personalities, and natural tendencies, we all perceive life and its many facets in a variety of ways. Sometimes I think it would be great if we could read minds. Well, if I could read *your* mind. I don't know how comfortable I'd be if you could read *mine!*

When we view another person as a potential threat to us—our safety, our family, our value, our reputation, our business, our ministry—we are forced to respond. Our response will depend greatly on the level of that threat. It has been said that our perception is our reality. This reveals to some extent the power of perception, don't you think? So it makes sense that some people would be more challenging to get along with. If either one of us perceives the other as a threat, how will we be able to trust each other in a relationship?

Does a particular person come to your mind as you read this? If so, who is it, and why does he/she come to your mind?

When we perceive a threat, our tendency is to find someone else who will join forces with us. We want an ally in case the threat should escalate into a conflict or confrontation. This can come in different forms:

- Gossip: We get on the phone or start a chat about how so-and-so is acting and how we think she needs to straighten up and fly right. We want to have someone else, someone we trust, in on this with us so that we feel validated in our response to the perceived threat.

- Rejection: We decide together that it is us against her. We want to know that if we all end up in the same place at the same time, we will not be the one who ends up alone.

- Surprise attack: If she doesn't see our attack coming, we can win the next battle and feel victorious. We decide together that we'll initiate conversations and engagements so that we're the ones holding all the cards.

You can probably think of other methods we use to forge these alliances, but they all boil down to a term I've learned from my husband, the counselor. It is called negative bonding, and it is destructive!

Negative bonding happens anytime two or more people form an alliance *against* any other person. This can happen in families—and often does. Sometimes one child will try to form an alliance with one parent against the other, or with one sibling against another.

There is a vivid illustration of this in the Old Testament. In Genesis 27, we read about a major turning point for the grandchildren of Abraham. Abraham's son, Isaac (the one God promised to give him in his old age), had married a woman named Rebekah. For a long time she was unable to conceive, but after time and many prayers she gave birth to twins: Jacob and Esau. Although the boys were twins, they were nothing alike. Esau loved hunting and the outdoors and connected most with his dad. Jacob preferred the indoors and hanging out at home and was closer to his mom.

As the boys grew up, Rebekah began "negative bonding" with Jacob.

I don't know how or when it first started, but it becomes clear in Genesis 27 that this was not an unusual relationship dynamic within Isaac's household. Rebekah was bound and determined that Jacob was going to receive the blessing which belonged to Esau, the older twin. Esau was heading out to hunt one day when Isaac had gotten so old that his eyes were beginning to fail him. He made a request that Esau bring him some stew from his hunt in time for Isaac to give him the fatherly blessing belonging to his firstborn. Rebekah overheard the conversation and decided to take action. Let's eavesdrop on the conversation, shall we?

> When Esau left for the open country to hunt game and bring it back, Rebekah said to her son Jacob, "Look, I overheard your father say to your brother Esau, 'Bring me some game and prepare me some tasty food to eat, so that I may give you my blessing in the presence of the LORD before I die.' Now, my son, listen carefully and do what I tell you: Go out to the flock and bring me two choice young goats, so I can prepare some tasty food for your father, just the way he likes it. Then take it to your father to eat, so that he may give you his blessing before he dies."

The Bible goes on to tell us that with little convincing, Rebekah got Jacob to go along with her little plot of deception. The irony is that this was completely unnecessary. God had already told them that Jacob would receive the greater blessing even though he was not the firstborn son. Strange things happen when we choose to form negative alliances rather than trusting our sovereign God. Jacob received his father's blessing, but it cost him dearly.

When have you seen or experienced negative bonding?

Real Threats

But what about the times when the perceived threat turns into an actualized, experienced threat…or worse? What about the times when those threats turn into actual wrongs committed against us? When we've been deceived? When someone has stolen from us? When someone has wounded us in some way or another? When someone wounds those we love? When we're taken advantage of? When the same person mistreats us over and over again? When we're victims of crimes? What then? Is peace still possible?

In 1999, I went through a very difficult season which actually was the culmination of several difficult seasons. At 25 years of age I found myself divorced with two little girls to raise as a single mom. It was painful enough to deal with the deterioration and dissolution of my marriage—the death of a dream—but it was even more excruciating to accept that another person—*another woman*—was now a part of my daughters' lives and there was nothing I could do about it. Part of me wanted to be a woman of honor and take the high road. The other part wanted to find her in a parking lot somewhere and snatch her bald-headed. I'd love to tell you that I immediately forgave her and trusted God with the situation, but I didn't.

It hurt so much.

Never before had I experienced such a betrayal or such a challenge to obey God's call to forgive.

Here is a story Jesus told about forgiveness:

> Peter got up the nerve to ask, "Master, how many times do I forgive a brother or sister who hurts me? Seven?" Jesus replied, "Seven! Hardly. Try seventy times seven. The kingdom of God is like a king who decided to square accounts with his servants. As he got under way, one servant was brought before him who had run up a debt of a hundred thousand dollars. He couldn't pay up, so the king ordered the man, along with his wife, children, and goods, to be auctioned off at the slave market. The poor wretch threw himself at the king's feet and begged, 'Give me a chance

and I'll pay it all back.' Touched by his plea, the king let him off, erasing the debt. The servant was no sooner out of the room when he came upon one of his fellow servants who owed him ten dollars. He seized him by the throat and demanded, 'Pay up. Now!' The poor wretch threw himself down and begged, 'Give me a chance and I'll pay it all back.' But he wouldn't do it. He had him arrested and put in jail until the debt was paid. When the other servants saw this going on, they were outraged and brought a detailed report to the king. The king summoned the man and said, 'You evil servant! I forgave your entire debt when you begged me for mercy. Shouldn't you be compelled to be merciful to your fellow servant who asked for mercy?' The king was furious and put the screws to the man until he paid back his entire debt" (Matthew 18:21-34 MSG).

Seventy Times Seven

When the topic of forgiveness comes up, I've often heard people say something like, "If you only knew what I went through because of that person, you'd understand why I can't forgive her." I've been the person on both sides of this equation. I think it is safe to say that's true for us all.

It is absolutely vital that we come to terms with how God views forgiveness and why He calls us to be people who forgive.

Principle 5: Choose Forgiveness

If I'm going to do all I can do to live at peace with everyone, I must learn to forgive.

God was gently working on my heart and used this passage in Matthew 18 to help me see that my fear of forgiving was based on a misunderstanding of biblical forgiveness. Let me explain.

- I understood forgiveness to mean that by forgiving her, I was declaring that what she did didn't really matter or hurt that much. I felt as though I was saying, "What you did to me was no big deal." But it *was* a very big deal!

- I believed—wrongly—that in forgiving her, I was letting her off the hook for what she did. As though my forgiveness had the power to release her from the natural consequences of her own choices.

- I was afraid that if I forgave her, it would give her the idea I liked her now. Like somehow I'd have to be willing to go have coffee with her or shop for my girls together or something.

Thankfully, God used this passage and some great truth-tellers in my life to help me get this whole muddy mess cleared up.

As you read the parable Jesus taught His followers, do you see Him minimize the reality of the debt owed at any time? No. In fact, He acknowledges that a debt is owed and that payment is expected. Remember that woman at the beginning of the book? God showed me that the debt this woman owed me was huge—so huge there was no way she could ever pay me back or make it right. You know why? Because the only way she could "fix" this or pay it back was to create a time machine, go back in time, and never cause pain to my family in the first place. I came to realize that even if she wanted to, she *couldn't* pay me back. The only way to clean the slate was if I relinquished my right to require her to pay me back. Through God's grace, I was able to recognize the futility of my unforgiveness in this regard.

Secondly, this parable helped me grasp that if I kept her attached to a hook, I was also attached to the same hook right next to her. I had to accept that by choosing to keep her connected to the line (hooked), I was actually keeping myself hooked. I don't know if you've ever gotten caught by a fishing hook, but it hurts! Refusing to forgive someone increases and sustains my own pain. Everywhere I went, every thought I had, every relationship in my life would find her influence present because I took her everywhere I went. Forgiving her released *me*. It got *me* off the hook!

And thirdly, I came to understand that none of this meant I had to enter into a relationship with her. Forgiveness and trust are not the same thing. Because of her lack of repentance or remorse for her actions that brought painful consequences (which, quite frankly, my family and I still experience), I could forgive without feeling the pressure to trust.

What about you? Do you identify with the above struggles to forgive someone in particular or in general?

If you are struggling to forgive someone, what is holding you back?

There is a difference between forgiving someone and trusting that someone. How would you communicate this idea to someone else?

Not only did God, in His perfect time and wisdom, reveal to me the power of genuine forgiveness, but He also reminded me that I can trust Him to deal with those who have wronged me.

Trust and Obey

There was a woman several years back who felt that I had wronged her, and she made everyone around us aware of this fact—and yet she never came to me personally to talk about it. She accused me of things

I had never done and did her best to tarnish my reputation. It was so hard for me to obey God's and my husband's direction to not go to her to straighten things out and to protect my reputation from the onslaught of these ugly accusations. It takes wisdom, humility, and patience to know when to confront someone and when to wait on the Lord. This was a long and challenging season of waiting.

Mutual friends came to me on occasion and asked me if what she was saying to them was true—just in case. I was able to speak directly with them and share that, although I'm far from perfect, these accusations were unfounded. Three or four years went by and even though things died down some, every time I saw her at church I was still aware that she was the one who had spread such ugly untruths about me. But over time God enabled me to let it go and not require that she pay me back…or even apologize. I can only explain this as the work of the Holy Spirit inside of me!

One day she caught me by surprise when she asked if she could speak with me alone. I had *no* idea what I was walking into! But to my great relief, surprise, and delight, she sincerely and humbly apologized. All those years before she had viewed (perceived) me as a threat and responded out of that fear. I am happy to say that we've seen each other many times over the years since and it is always a pleasant experience. Only God could work in the hearts and lives of two of His children like this!

I learned through this whole ordeal that God will not ever take from one of His children to give to another. So when we see someone receiving or experiencing something that we long to have ourselves, we need to remember that God is, by nature, trustworthy and good. If I had jumped the gun to protect my own reputation or to say my piece, there is a good chance things would have turned out badly. Sometimes God isn't calling us to confront, but to wait on Him to work. He does a far better job than we do, so it is always a good idea to listen to Him and simply trust and obey. Wouldn't you agree?

Personal Response

What about you? Have you experienced a similar situation—on either end of the spectrum? Share what you experienced, how you responded, and what God taught you.

Think back to the story of Rebekah and Isaac and their sons, Jacob and Esau. When have you observed negative bonding within families? How does this impact everyone involved?

Are you dealing with someone who perceives you as a threat? How are you handling the situation?

Dear heavenly Father, thank You for the countless times that You have shown me what being forgiven feels like. By Your grace, and in Your strength, please embolden me to display this character trait in my life as well. In Jesus's name, amen.

12

Conflict and Confrontation

The truth may be painful, but it should never be hurtful.
REV. JAMES EUBANKS

Revenge can feel so empowering, but genuine strength is revealed when we take that power we have over others and, instead of giving in to the screaming emotions that demand vindication, make a choice to live out of who God says we are. Here is what a friend of mine shared with me about making a tough choice to offer love instead of taking revenge on someone who had wounded her:

> About a year before I met, dated, and married my husband, I was dating a guy named John. I thought he was perfect. He was tall, dark, and handsome. He was from my hometown and he was a minister at the church I'd attended when I was little. I thought it was a match made in heaven. We did the long-distance dating thing for about six months and I thought it was great.
>
> One weekend he asked me to come home so I could go to his best friend's wedding (for whom he was a groomsman).

The whole weekend he was sweet, romantic, and wonderful…and I let my guard down. I allowed him to go a little bit further physically with me then I had intended, but I thought "Hey, we're moving in the marriage direction (I thought!), so I can go to second or third base and it won't be a problem!" Little did I know what was up ahead in the next few days!

I came home from the romantic weekend on a Saturday night. The next day he called and suggested meeting at a local mall halfway between our homes the following week. Of course I said yes! I got so excited about seeing him!

We met and had a great date. But then, as he walked me to my car, he dumped me! Out of the blue! I was devastated. Not only because I was heartbroken, but because I felt very used! I was so mad and really thought about getting him in trouble with his boss. I knew many of the members at the church where he was on staff, and some of the deacons and elders were great friends of our family. All I had to do was make a few phone calls, shed a few tears, and he would be out of a job. Believe me, I thought about it.

But then I remembered someone telling me that "Forgiveness is not saying that the person who wronged you is right. Forgiveness frees you up to move on to bigger and better things that God has in store for you." I realized that throwing a fit, gossiping, and damaging my ex's reputation would not make my hurt and used feelings go away. So I didn't do anything. I let it go and just went on with my life.

Just a few months later, when my heart was still a little tender from the break-up, my wonderful husband (of six years now) walked into my life! I am thankful that I chose the high road and allowed God to speak to my heart and live His life through my own!

In my friend's life, can you see how things could have gone so differently if she had been wrapped up in a quest for vengeance rather than allowing herself to be open to whatever God had in mind? I can totally identify with her story. When I went through my divorce, I was tempted—oh, was I tempted!—to seek revenge, to get even, to make him pay. But then God stepped in. Because I had been intentional with His Word for so long, there was already a foundation of truth that wouldn't budge during that intense storm in my life. If I had held onto my pride, I would not have been in any shape to begin a new life with Stephen when he came my way.

Forgiveness and Confrontation

What about the times when God reveals to you that you need to confront and not let something go on any longer? To someone like me who avoids conflict, this is a source of some major anxiety! I would rather walk on hot coals than confront someone about a conflict. Confrontation is a risk, and I don't enjoy it! Sometimes it feels spiritual to let ourselves believe that we have forgiven someone so there's no need to confront them.

Some people live for conflict. They can usually be seen initiating debates, stirring up arguments just for the sake of being heard, and rocking a gently floating boat. I know people like this, but I'll probably never understand them. I appreciate their boldness when they filter it through respect for others, but most of my experiences have been with those who enjoyed mowing people down just for the fun of it.

After a decade of dealing with the woman who "starred" in the first story of this book, God finally began to nudge me towards confrontation with her. I had already spent years praying for the relationship, praying for her, asking God what was wrong with me, inviting a few safe and trusted people to share with me if there was something about me that could be offensive to others, and repeatedly wondering, "Why can't we just get along?" I had spent many seasons over that decade avoiding her and giving up on any kind of reconciliation of the relationship. Forgiving her was one thing; giving her permission to continue her abuse was another.

Every time I began to think things were beginning to get a little better, she'd blindside me with a very hurtful and offensive comment or action. She criticized me. She criticized my husband and children. She insulted the ministry God has entrusted to me. I began to realize that, for some reason, she perceived me as a threat. With that in mind I tried to minimize any talk about myself, my family, and the ministry and get engaged in conversation about what was happening in her life and in her family. None of this worked. So eventually, God went from a gentle nudge to talk with her to a full-blown, I-will-not-let-you-sleep-or-take-another-step-forward-until-you-do *shove* to open up the dialogue with her about this.

Through the wisdom my husband shared with me and the nudging—er, shoving—of the Holy Spirit, I began to realize that I needed to confront this woman regardless of how she responded to it. God wanted me to obey, not to win. He showed me that my obedience to Him in trust was my only concern, not the end result. Of course I wanted a peaceful resolution, but I couldn't choose obedience based on a predicted outcome.

So with much fear and trembling, I set up a coffee date with her so that I could give her an opportunity to share with me, personally and privately, if I had done something to offend her in some way, to ask for and offer forgiveness where necessary, and to stop the cycle that was bordering on abusive to me and to my children.

I am not exaggerating when I say I did this with fear and trembling. I wanted to obey God and trust Him for the outcome, but I also wanted her to back out of the whole thing! I was afraid I'd say something wrong or start crying and appear weak and vulnerable (to someone who had already hurt me over and over again for years) or worse—throw up at the table! I was afraid because I feared that this would make an already difficult relationship even worse based on how she might choose to respond.

I sat down and asked her, "Have I offended you in some way that would give you the desire to hurt me back?" In our conversation she told me that I had not done anything to her and she wasn't sure why she treated me like she had for so many years. At first she was defensive, which was to be expected—I had had time to pray and think through what I was going to say; she didn't know the coffee talk was going to be like this.

To her credit, she came around and apologized. And I set some necessary boundaries with her right then and there. Remember, forgiveness and trust are not twins. I knew I could forgive her, but I also knew that I wasn't ready to trust her. I let her know that if she insulted me or my family that I would call her on it right when it happened and wouldn't pretend any longer. She accepted the boundary. We were able to end the confrontation with hugs, a few tears, and—finally—peace.

I sometimes wonder if that was a conversation I should have had long before. Before my children were wounded by the words of an adult who should have known better. Before I got to the place where having that conversation would nearly have me in hives. But regardless, I'm glad I finally sat down to talk! No, this woman and I are not close friends even years after the conversation. But we can be in the same place at the same time and we can enjoy our mutual relationships with ease and respect.

Do you tend to initiate confrontation fairly easily or avoid it at all costs? Why do you think you handle conflict this way?

"As much as is possible"

Unfortunately, it is just not going to be possible to be at peace with everyone in every situation. I am so thankful the apostle Paul acknowledges this. There are so many wounded adults in the world—and in the Church—who are grappling with what biblical forgiveness looks like when it comes to a person who has either passed away or still poses a threat. God may call us to walk a path that hurts us in some way, but only for our greater good. But He will never call us to do something that will *harm us*. I have told my children many times that as a mom I might have to *hurt* them (like taking them to get shots at the doctor's office), but I will never intentionally *harm* them. My desire is that they trust my heart is for them always.

So what should we do, what *can* we do, when we cannot make peace with another person for either of these reasons? What if the one who wounded us so deeply was a parent or grandparent who has passed away and cannot understand how their actions have pained us? How do we handle the person who, for whatever reason, poses a risk to our personal safety?

My husband, Stephen, deals with this kind of reality every single day. He is the Director of Clinical Programs for a ministry he cofounded called HopeQuest Ministry Group(www.hqmg.org). HopeQuest is a Christ-centered recovery facility for men and women who struggle with life-dominating issues. In Stephen's practice as a counselor and teacher, he often leads clients to write a letter to the one who wronged them—or perhaps the one they wronged—who can no longer communicate with them for the reasons listed above. Expressing the emotions, clarifying the thoughts, and writing down the words is a powerful and practical way to do *your part* to be at peace with everyone, even those whom you might never be able to confront or communicate with in person. Stephen also recommends burning the letter(s) when you're done!

I was at a conference years ago when Beth Moore had just started speaking at arena-sized events for women. I'll never forget her words on this very topic. She said a very wise thing which has stayed with me all these years and has helped me make some really tough choices in relationship struggles. She said that sometimes God's grace will lead us to reconciliation with another person *through* the cross of Christ and to the other person so that the relationship can be restored. And sometimes God's grace will lead us to reconciliation *to* the cross of Christ, and no further, protecting us (and perhaps the other person as well) from relationship with each other. We need to remember that we still live in a broken, flawed, fallen world and we still deal with our own human weaknesses that prevent us, at least for a while, from being in a position to reconcile with every person. Sometimes finding peace means finding it in my relationship with Christ and in placing the other person in His far wiser and more capable hands.

All of this takes wisdom and guidance from the Holy Spirit. I have found that the biblical principle of seeking wise counsel before making big decisions is definitely required here. When confronting, I have brought in voices of grace and truth who were not emotionally connected to the situations to benefit from their wise counsel and from their earnest prayers for me. Peace is possible for us all through Christ, but peace *with* everyone may not be possible—completely—within this lifetime.

Do you have a situation in your life that calls for a letter-writing session? Don't feel pressured to do this today or right away, and definitely don't feel pressured to do this completely alone. Bring in someone safe who can walk with you if necessary.

Why do you think God chooses to reconcile some of us *through* the cross of Christ and some of us *to* the cross of Christ? What might make the latter necessary?

"Do all that you can to live at peace with everyone."

This biblical mandate doesn't ask of us the impossible. It doesn't ask us to play God or try to be a god to anyone. It doesn't ask us to be perfect. It reveals the ability we have to make a greater impact for good in our generation.

Whenever we're riddled with guilt or bitterness or regret, we remain shackled in chains that have already been unlocked for us. But it has always been and will always be our choice to remain in those shackles or to cast them off and run in the freedom purchased for us by the forgiveness of God. He set things right. He initiated the forgiveness of all of our wrongs toward Him. And He is the One who makes us able to offer that kind of forgiveness to others, whether they realize they need it or not.

One final thought: Whenever we see that a confrontation is necessary, it is vital that we first take the time needed to examine our own hearts and motives. The importance of this cannot be overstated, so please take the time to do this thoroughly by answering these questions:

1. **What is my motive in confronting this other person or group?** If your answer reveals a desire for revenge, to put the other person in his or her place, or something of that flavor, please wait until your emotions have calmed down enough to handle the confrontation with respect for the other person.

2. **Am I ready to accept that the other person may not respond the way I would prefer?** Take the time to release your expectations and desires to your heavenly Father. Going into the confrontation with an agenda can put both you and the other person on the defensive if things don't go your way.

3. **Is this safe?** Not to be melodramatic, but the truth is that some confrontations are unwise because the emotions involved can escalate, putting one or both people at risk for harm—either verbally or physically. If it isn't safe, don't

confront (or don't go it alone). Common sense applies here.

4. **What do I hope to gain?** If you recognize that the importance is that your voice be heard, and not that the other person respond in the way you desire, then you are probably ready to confront.

Remember: The truth may be painful, but it should never be hurtful. Check your motives, investigate your desires, evaluate your safety, and acknowledge your hopes before heading into a confrontation with another person. I believe these steps will help you to get your thoughts together for a respectful confrontation with just about anyone. (*Just* about!)

Personal Response

Conflict and confrontation can be so challenging. From what you read in this chapter, and from your own understanding, what elements are crucial to a healthy handling of confrontation?

What is God showing you? How will you respond?

Dear heavenly Father, confrontation can be so difficult for us. Please remind us when we feel overloaded that Your yoke is easy and Your burden is light. May we cast our burdens upon Your capable shoulders and may we trust You to take good care of those things which concern us and those we love. You are able. Help us to trust You. In Jesus's name, amen.

13

Grace Under Fire

You can't have peace if you don't understand grace.
JOYCE MEYER

Throughout this book, you and I have been walking together on a journey towards finding peace in all of our relationships. This is no small feat to achieve! I applaud you for staying with this book into these final chapters. Take a moment to pat yourself on the back for me, okay?

Let's review the principles we've covered so far:

1. Principle 1: Offer yourself as a living sacrifice by being intentional with God's Word and by willingly humbling yourself before God and others.

2. Principle 2: Accept and appreciate the differences you see in others.

3. Principle 3: Live out of who God says you are.

4. Principle 4: Choose your friends wisely.

5. Principle 5: Choose forgiveness.

As we seek to become people who do all that we can do to live at peace with everyone we encounter, we must take biblical principles to heart. These are the God-breathed principles that stand the test of time.

When we apply the truths found in Romans 12 (and other passages of Scripture) to our lives and relationships, we're going to find that there is one major theme throughout the pages of the Bible and throughout the scenes of history. This theme is Grace!

Principle 6: Become a Dispenser of Grace

Kill 'em with kindness?

Remember, our key verse is Romans 12:18: "If it is possible, as far as it depends on you, live at peace with everyone." We've discussed several principles that will equip us to do our part to live at peace with everyone. I believe peace is possible in almost all of our relationships, but I do understand that there are exceptions to this. In those exceptions, we can be at peace, even if the relationship itself cannot.

This passage in Romans goes on to say in verses 19-21,

> Do not take revenge, my dear friends, but leave room for God's wrath, for it is written: "It is mine to avenge; I will repay," says the Lord. On the contrary: "If your enemy is hungry, feed him; if he is thirsty, give him something to drink. In doing this, you will heap burning coals on his head." Do not be overcome by evil, but overcome evil with good.

Hmmm…I've always kind of liked that whole "heap burning coals on their heads" part of this passage. It makes me feel like less of a victim knowing I have this option to choose from now and again…But we'll come back to this later. Hang tight!

Grace That Is Greater

God's grace means more to me today than it ever did when I was growing up and attending different churches. Back then I understood that God's grace meant that if we accepted Jesus Christ as our Lord and

Savior, repented of our sins, and placed our faith in Him, we would go to heaven when we died and not have to go to hell. I guess I figured that between the two choices, the first was the only logical one to make.

Most of what I knew back then was that if you were a Christian, you stood *against* a whole lot of things. Although we did experience some really good times, it was far from "joy inexpressible and full of glory" (1 Peter 1:8 NKJV). I was afraid almost all of the time. Afraid because I knew that God was watching every single thing I did and He was keeping a record of it all. I was afraid of Him because I only knew Him to be powerful and mostly angry—because we as His people were always messing up. I imagined that He was expecting *me* to mess up. And if He was expecting it, then I was in for it when it actually happened. He was prepared.

What were your earliest views of God? How did you picture Him when you were a child?

I can't tell you how many times I heard someone, usually an adult in the church, say, "Shelley, I can't believe you did that—you're the pastor's daughter!" (They didn't seem to notice or care that whatever it was I was doing, I was doing with *their* kid!) I didn't know the God who made Himself known to us in the person of Jesus Christ. To me, the two personalities couldn't have been more different from each other.

In the church environments I was familiar with, our relationship with God was mostly focused on the rules we needed to keep: stay away from secular music and movies, don't go to public schools, don't play cards, don't wear a two-piece bathing suit, don't swim with the opposite sex, don't…don't…don't…the list could go on and on. In fact, I heard of one college student (at a Christian college) who was not allowed to graduate with his class because he talked to his fiancée in public with-out a chaperone present. Yes. Really. I also heard of a church that keeps a barber's chair in the foyer to cut the hair of men who might just show up to church with their hair touching their collar or ears. Yes. Really. And these two stories aren't pulled from the 1950s either.

Now I know things have changed a lot in the culture and climate of *most* of today's churches. Most of us realize that even with the best of intentions, legalism stifles our growth as Christians. God doesn't initi-ate this kind of relationship with people!

But of course there's an opposite extreme as well. It is almost weird in some Christian churches for someone to show up in a suit and tie carrying a Bible. In those churches, people in jeans and T-shirts read the Bible on their iPhones and make critical remarks about those who are so "old school."

For goodness' sake, we wear the same name, so *why can't we all just get along?* For the sake of ourselves, and especially for those who have *never* had a positive experience with those who claim that Name, we've got to do better. And we can!

The truth about God's grace to us

If God's grace is even bigger than getting us to heaven—which, by the way, is no small matter—how can we hope to understand or explain it?

Some have used the following acronym:

God's
Riches
At
Christ's
Expense

Consider what my friend Cindy Beall shares about her understand-ing of grace:

> Good old Webster's defines grace as "unmerited, divine assistance given humans for their regeneration or sancti-fication." Here is how I reworded the phrase to help me

better grasp what God was trying to say to me: "My unmerited, divine assistance given to you is enough." [7]

My son is in Cub Scouts. In the Scouts, there are badges he can earn. These are called "merit badges." He doesn't get these simply because he goes to the meetings, because he is so likable, or even because he wants them really badly. He has to prove he has earned them. And wisely so. There are some things in life that need to be earned. But grace is unique. Grace is something that is *unmerited*, which means that we can't earn it, can't do anything to deserve it. The bottom line is this: If it can be earned it ceases to be grace!

In your own words, how would you define grace?

> Does the God who lavishly provides you with his own presence, his Holy Spirit, working things in your lives you could never do for yourselves, does he do these things because of your strenuous moral striving or because you trust him to do them in you? Don't these things happen among you just as they happened with Abraham? He believed God, and that act of belief was turned into a life that was right with God (Galatians 3:5-6 MSG).

Grace is experienced through our trust in the One who offers it. And the other reality is this: According to Scripture, which reveals to us God's nature and character, the Creator of this world delights in offering grace to those of us who humbly respond to Him and simply receive it.

This is how much God loved the world: He gave his Son,

his one and only Son. And this is why: so that no one need be destroyed; by believing in him, anyone can have a whole and lasting life. God didn't go to all the trouble of sending his Son merely to point an accusing finger, telling the world how bad it was. He came to help, to put the world right again. Anyone who trusts in him is acquitted; anyone who refuses to trust him has long since been under the death sentence without knowing it. And why? Because of that person's failure to believe in the one-of-a-kind Son of God when introduced to him (John 3:16-18 MSG).

These passages are only two of the many, many passages of Scripture that reveal the goodness and gracious nature of God. He is a God who makes the broken whole. He is the God who makes the powerless triumphant. He is the God who transforms the ugly into the radiant. He is so good and He is so full of grace! And He delights in our trust in Him!

How would you describe your relationship with God?

The truth about our grace to others

In all of the stories I've shared in this book about girls and teens and women hurting other girls and teens and women, I hope you've noticed a thread woven through each and every one of them, tying them all together. That thread is brokenness. Actually that thread is *unresolved* brokenness. Because truth be told, as long as we're alive and

> Grace to me is God's power flowing through me as I yield my life to Him.
>
> —Jeanette, Texas

well on Planet Earth, we'll all still be at least somewhat broken. None of us gets to have "perfect" in the here and now.

So what are we to do?

Receive grace.

Offer grace.

The obstacle that stands between my natural human response to pain (avoiding it at all costs and getting revenge on the one who hurts me) and my desire to live the way God calls me to (offering grace, mercy, and forgiveness) is my own understanding of who I am and whose I am. Because this truth remains: I can't offer someone anything I don't possess myself. I doubt my neighbors would appreciate me giving you *their* nice new SUV. I don't have one to give you, so you will not be getting one from me. Same goes for grace. If I haven't received grace and embraced grace, then I do not have any grace to offer to you, and I can't take someone else's to give to you. I can only give to you out of my own resources and supply.

You and I who are believers in Jesus Christ already have what it takes to offer grace to others. Second Peter 1:3 tells us that "His divine power has given us everything we need for a godly life through our knowledge of him who called us by his own glory and goodness." We have been given everything we need that pertains to living a godly life. That's a big deal. And as we make the choice to regularly and intentionally remember who we belong to, what He has done for us, and what He equips us to do by *His* grace, we will find ourselves better able to draw from that grace placed in us in order that we can then dispense it to those around us.

> Under grace God blesses us with everything in Christ and through the blessings empowers us to obey Him.
>
> —Linda, Georgia

Let's take another look at what Paul said in Romans 12:19-21:

> Do not take revenge, my dear friends, but leave room for God's wrath, for it is written: "It is mine to avenge; I will repay," says the Lord. On the contrary: "If your enemy is

hungry, feed him; if he is thirsty, give him something to drink. In doing this, you will heap burning coals on his head." Do not be overcome by evil, but overcome evil with good.

God's Word tells us that when we have been wronged by someone, when we feel ourselves pulling our hair and crying out in desperation, we can receive God's divine assistance (which we cannot earn) in order to offer it to those who inflict pain upon us. We don't get to pay them back; God is the only One with the authority to seek revenge. I think this is because He is the only One who can see the whole picture—beginning, middle, end, and everything surrounding it. We don't have this kind of insight.

Think about it: Only God can be angry and, in His anger, still do the right thing for the circumstance and relationship. Only God! When you or I get overly emotional—joyful, excited, happy, sad, angry, or depressed—we need to be cautious. We have all made choices we regret, and most of the time it was because we made a decision in the heat of emotion (positive or negative) that we shouldn't have made until the emotion had a chance to settle down. This is how salespeople make their quotas, by the way: They get the buyer hyped up emotionally in order to close the sale right away. You probably won't hear a salesperson say, "Why don't you take some time to think this through carefully before you sign the contract?"

Have you made a decision or a purchase you later regretted because you did so during the height of emotion? Share your experience.

So although God does experience emotions, including anger, He says, "Let Me handle the vengeance. Your job is to feed your hungry enemy and overcome evil with good." This comes into conflict with our own natural tendencies. After all, we want revenge when we've been wronged. So why does God tell us we should feed and care for our enemies? Because in doing this, you will "heap burning coals on his head." *What?* Seriously, stop and consider how ironic this sounds. Offer grace by setting their hair on fire? Really?

I've been taught for years that this is where the line about "killing 'em with kindness" comes from. That killing someone with kindness is actually biblical. In fact, I heard this not too long ago from a pastor I greatly admire and respect. I just happen to disagree with him. (So much so that I could picture myself interrupting him right then and there to set him straight. I'm so glad I didn't do that.) Here's why I felt so passionate about this topic:

Several years ago I heard something powerful that shifted my whole mental image and radically changed my motives for showing kindness to those who have wronged me. I learned to read this Scripture the way the original readers would have understood it! Those readers would have had a very specific picture in mind when they heard this verse. Since times have changed a lot since then, we need the historical background to help us "see" as well. (Scripture is full of treasure for those who are willing to do a little extra digging—it is so worth it!)

In biblical days, homes were built differently from our houses today. Because there was nothing like electricity or central heating and air, people had to be a little more creative in how they structured their living spaces. Instead of windows with glass panes which could be opened and closed or covered and uncovered with window treatments like we enjoy today, the people of those days lived in homes with smaller windows which were placed closer to the roof of the home. This allowed for ventilation of the home and also offered greater privacy for those within the home.

At one point in the day, the poorer people in the village were allowed to carry a bucket or something similar on the tops of their heads as they walked under the windows of the homes in order to receive much-needed coal to warm their water, cook their food, and bathe their families. Everyone needed coal, but not everyone had the ability to get their own. Those who had generous hearts would "heap burning coals" on the heads of those who didn't have the ability to get this commodity on their own. This is grace! It wasn't a matter of whether or not the people receiving the coal had earned it. It was a matter of grace on the parts of those who offered it to those who couldn't (or wouldn't) do anything for them in return.

Other translations use the term "burning coals of shame," and I want to address this as well. Remember, God speaks in one voice and it is always a voice reflecting His love, truth, and grace. There is a difference in someone feeling ashamed of their actions, attitudes, and behaviors and in feeling shame because of who they are. One is better translated "guilt" than "shame." When we behave out of our true identities, lavishing gifts of grace to people who have wronged us, our love in action can be the catalyst for change in their lives as their sense of guilt prompts them to turn in the right direction. We need to be careful, though, about our motives for extending grace to others. God may want to use us as change agents, but we are not the ones responsible to change anyone. Therefore, our grace needs to be offered without any strings attached. Otherwise, these gifts turn into tools of manipulation. Been there. Done that. Ouch.

How does "heaping burning coals" on someone's head represent God's grace to us? And how does this equate to "overcoming evil with good?"

Isn't this a beautiful picture of God's amazing grace to us? He offers to us something that we can never earn. He lavishly bestows out of His divine treasury. He pours His grace on us and then invites us into this grace-giving way of life with Him. This beats revenge hands down! When we decide, once and for all, that we will become dispensers of the grace of God to those within our spheres of influence, it changes everything. Living this way is a big part of the abundant life Jesus came to give us (see John 10:10).

If I choose to show kindness to someone who has wronged me with the motive of "kill her with kindness," how in the world is this reflective of God's grace and the nature that He is developing and cultivating in me? The simple answer is that it isn't. Not even a little bit.

He Gives the Love Itself

As I prayerfully and thoughtfully considered what story to share here, I kept coming back to one of the most powerful stories I've ever heard on the subject of forgiveness and grace *given* rather than revenge *taken*.

Corrie ten Boom is a hero to believers the world over. As you are probably aware, Corrie's small family gave their all to protect Jews during the horror of the Holocaust. Their story is told in full in Corrie's book *The Hiding Place*. Corrie and her sister were placed in the same concentration camp once it was discovered that they were protecting so many Jews. In this concentration camp, the sisters, along with the others there, were raped repeatedly—among other horrors—during their time at the camp. Her sister, Betsie, died there. Corrie was released from the camp just a week before the rest of the women were killed. She found out later that her release had been a clerical error.

After her release, and after the war's end, God used Corrie to share the message of the gospel—God's grace and forgiveness—to many. Read her own words here about the time she was faced with the choice to either offer grace or take revenge:

> It was at a church service in Munich that I saw him, the former S.S. man who had stood guard at the shower room door in the processing center at Ravensbruck. He was the first of our actual jailers that I had seen since that time. And

suddenly it was all there—the roomful of mocking men, the heaps of clothing, Betsie's pain-blanched face.

He came up to me as the church was emptying, beaming and bowing. "How grateful I am for your message, Fraulein," he said. "To think that, as you say, He has washed my sins away!"

His hand was thrust out to shake mine. And I, who had preached so often to the people in Bloemendaal the need to forgive, kept my hand at my side.

Even as the angry, vengeful thoughts boiled through me, I saw the sin of them. Jesus Christ had died for this man; was I going to ask for more? Lord Jesus, I prayed, forgive me and help me to forgive him.

I tried to smile, I struggled to raise my hand. I could not. I felt nothing, not the slightest spark of warmth or charity. And so again I breathed a silent prayer. Jesus, I cannot forgive him. Give me Your forgiveness.

As I took his hand the most incredible thing happened. From my shoulder along my arm and through my hand a current seemed to pass from me to him, while into my heart sprang a love for this stranger that almost overwhelmed me.

And so I discovered that it is not on our forgiveness any more than on our goodness that the world's healing hinges, but on His. When He tells us to love our enemies, He gives, along with the command, the love itself. [8]

Kill 'em with kindness? I think not. I think God's grace shown to us and then through us is a whole lot bigger—and better!—than that!

> The truth may require a scalpel, but it will never require a knife.
>
> —Andy Stanley

Personal Response

How does this understanding of Romans 12:19-21 change your perspective as it pertains to "killing them with kindness"?

How does this understanding impact our motives for showing kindness to those who have wronged us?

Dear heavenly Father, Your grace still amazes me! To think that the Creator, Sustainer, and Ruler of the whole world would humble Himself to the point of extending His unmerited favor on my life is a thought too great for my mind to comprehend fully. All I can do is give You everything—all that I have and all that I am—in return. It all comes from Your hand anyway! Make me a vessel, a conduit of Your grace to others, I pray. And for those times when I'll miss the mark yet again, thank You that Your grace covers me still! In Jesus's precious and powerful name, amen.

14

A Future Worth Looking Forward To

We should all be concerned about the future because we will have to spend the rest of our lives there.

CHARLES F. KETTERING

I remember it like it was yesterday. Once again, in the words of Job, "what I feared [had] come upon me" (Job 3:25). The closer the relationship, the greater the turmoil when something goes wrong. Just remembering it now causes the pain I felt then to resurface in my heart and mind. All hope seemed lost. My child was heading down a path that clearly led to destruction and I felt completely helpless to do anything about it.

I lost a lot of sleep during those dark days and I shed a lot of tears. I cried out to God in ways I had never even thought I could. I felt helpless. Hopeless. It is true that our greatest wounds come through relationships. I questioned myself as a mother, a woman, and as a child of God. How could this be happening?

Today as I hear parents share their angst and grief over choices made by their children, my heart immediately goes out to them. I don't think there is another pain quite like the pain of watching our children head in the wrong direction. At one point in that season of our lives, God whispered this phrase softly and tenderly to my spirit: *A future worth looking forward to*. I started to pray that God would show my daughter the kind of future He had for her and that the path she was currently skipping down was not leading to that desired end.

Remember, we don't live our lives, make our plans, spend our money, invest our time, or cultivate relationships based on who we are but on who we believe we are. I knew the truth of Proverbs 29:18: "If people can't see what God is doing, they stumble all over themselves; But when they attend to what he reveals, they are most blessed" (MSG). I wanted my child to get a glimpse of what God was doing in her life so that she would be able to embrace the blessings He had for her.

It isn't easy to help someone see this when they are wearing blinders, so I had to tread carefully and seek God's clear direction at every turn. There is no magic formula that can predict and guarantee the future any of us desire—for ourselves or for others—but there are principles, like the ones we've discussed here, that will help to ensure that we are building a sturdy foundation that will stand strong during the biggest storms of our lives. This foundation—these time-tested principles— help us have a future ahead of us that is worth looking forward to today.

If it is possible…

As far as it depends on you…

Every one of us can experience the Peace of Christ. It is in our best interest to make it a practice to apply these principles to our lives:

1. Offer yourself as a living sacrifice by being intentional with God's Word and by willingly humbling yourself before God and others.

2. Accept and appreciate the differences you see in others.

3. Live out of who God says you are.

4. Choose your friends wisely.

5. Choose forgiveness.

6. Become a dispenser of grace.

If we've learned nothing else in this journey together, we've at least acknowledged that our relationships are extremely significant, and that if we are going to experience peace—even in the most challenging of them all—we must recognize that ultimately, we cannot do this in our own power or strength or wisdom. Remember, "What man initiates, man must sustain; but what God initiates, God will sustain."

When we boil all of this down into one prevailing principle, it is this: Our responsibility as children of God is to live our lives based on our true identity regardless of what others do or how they live. No one can take this power away from you. You can surrender it, but it can't be taken from you.

The journey to discovering who we really are—as defined by our Creator, the only One with the power to define us—can be very painful. But the necessary pain to produce freedom is so worth it! Anyone on this side of that mountain will vouch for this reality. I'm comforted in the promise that our God will never leave us and will never forsake us (Deuteronomy 31:6). He remains with us through every twist and turn and is working everything together for our good (Romans 8:28).

As we turn the last corner of our journey together, I want to share with you some compelling reasons for taking the time to discover who we really are—according to God's Word—and to doing our part to live at peace with everyone. The path toward a better future begins with the steps we take today.

Our relationships have incredible significance.

Just today I received an email from a grown woman in her thirties who shared with me the negative impact her mother's words, spoken to her in childhood, still have on her today. Her mother's influence is the filter by which she sees herself and by which she measures her own success as a mom. Rather than loving and delighting in her daughter, her mother chose instead to compare my friend to her other daughter—the bright one, the pretty one, the one who did everything right. Constantly hearing the words "Why can't you be more like your sister?" has continued to haunt her even into adulthood.

But what if she were to begin applying these six principles in her life beginning now? How might this help her to find peace with her mother, regardless of whether or not her mother decides to change her script?

We've Got the Power!

If you are God's child through a relationship with His Son, Jesus Christ, then you have the Holy Spirit living inside of you. Pause for a minute to think about the implications of this miraculous truth. For some of us who have been Christians for a long time, we might read that quickly and then move on, but let's not just move on, okay? Let's give ourselves a minute to allow this truth to sink in more than ever before.

Name something really powerful that God has done whether in stories found in the Bible, in history, or in your own life. You might want to name more than one. If so, go for it!

Think about someone whose words can still be heard in your thoughts on a regular basis. Who was this person? What did he/she say that you can still hear (often)?

You and I—and everyone we will ever lay eyes upon—have been made in the image of God. His power is on display for all of us to see. He has done and continues to perform mighty acts! *And we are made in His image!* One facet of this incredible truth is that our words, like His, carry some serious weight. Our actions matter. Our decisions matter. What could happen if more of us realized this and began to live with the awareness that what we say has real and lasting power in the lives of others? What could have been different for the mother and daughter whose story I shared briefly just a few paragraphs back?

Counselors often have their clients create a two-column page with the headings: "My responsibilities" and "God's responsibilities." The purpose of this is to help individuals see in black and white where they might be trying to take on some roles and responsibilities that can only be fulfilled by their heavenly Father. This can be a helpful tool to help us see what is blocking the road to peace within our relationships. For example, one might realize that she has tried to control the outcome of her career by micromanaging every little detail to ensure that she is considered for a promotion, which she sees as a means to her own security. It is quite possible that her behavior is creating too many demands for others to fulfill and is also causing distress, rather than peace, within the context of both her professional and personal relationships. Perhaps what God desires is that she offer her best (not perfection, but quality) and trust that He will provide for her in His timing and in His own ways. This is just an example, but I think it makes the point that we often forget who the Source of our strength (i.e. power) really is.

Create a two-column list of what you are responsible for and what your heavenly Father is responsible for. It might help you discover what is keeping you from experiencing peace in relationships with others.

My Responsibilities   God's Responsibilities

Know what you have power over and have integrity with that.

We all *want* to have a future worth looking forward to, of course, but some of us are really fearful of the future. We've seen what can happen and we often fear what could happen to us. This is where understanding our own limitations and responsibilities comes to the rescue.

The woman described in Proverbs 31 was not fearful of the future. Perhaps she understood what Corrie ten Boom came to understand; that we should "Never be afraid to trust an unknown future to a known God." God is full of integrity. When I embrace this truth, it goes a long way toward reducing my fears.

> She is clothed with strength and dignity; she can laugh at the days to come (Proverbs 31:25).

Know what you have power over and be full of integrity with that. What exactly is integrity? I think the best definition I've ever seen explained it this way: Integrity is when…

my thoughts = my words = my actions

When my life is "integrated" and consistent, I can be described as a person of integrity. Trusting God's integrity—that His thoughts = His words = His actions—enables me to be a person of integrity as well.

Rest in God's power to handle what He is responsible to handle, including the future. He is already there. We are not. In the situation with my daughter, my responsibility was to help her envision a future worth looking forward to—through my words, my actions, and my unconditional love towards her. It was God's job to bring about life change. It was her job to decide whether or not to receive what was offered to her. I'm so thankful that she did. It didn't happen overnight, but it did happen. And I'm thankful for the peace God allowed me to experience during that difficult season when the future was completely unknown to me.

Woman—you have some serious power!

I learned a long time ago that as women, we have a lot of power. We can use this power to get what we want a lot of the time—but do we really? I mean, do we really get what we want? I can manipulate, control, demand, insist, and plead to get what I want when I want it. I can do all of this to *convince* those in my life to do what I want. But you know what I've learned is a lot better for all concerned? When I back off of God's responsibilities and I allow His Spirit, in His perfect time and way, to bring about conviction that lasts. What I do to convince can be undone in mere seconds. But when God's Spirit brings conviction…that's a whole other story!

When you face the difficult people in your life and have to deal with the relationship woes that are a part of life, remember, you've got some serious power. But also remember that it needs to be used wisely. I'm sure you've heard meekness described as "power under control." When we as women allow the power God has given to us to be under His control, it makes us absolutely radiant!

You and God are the only common denominators in every one of your relationships.

At the time of this writing, both of my girls are learning to drive. One is more of a natural at it than the other. (I told you they are complete opposites.) Just the other day, we were at a family gathering and the one who isn't as strong behind the wheel was commenting on how each of her parents—mom, dad, and stepdad—were nervous when riding with her, but for no reason. Her uncle quietly replied, "And what is the one common denominator in all of this?"

It is true that I am a common denominator in all of my relationships. But because Christ is in me, *God and I* are the only common denominators in *all* of my relationships.

Now, let *that one* sink in for a minute!

Just look at your Facebook profile and you will see that we all have a lot of mutual relationships.

> And this is the secret: Christ lives in you (Colossians 1:27 NLT).

It is kind of like the whole "Six degrees of separation" game. But God is the only One who is a part of *all* of our other relationships. This means that He brings His nature to those friendships as well. I can experience peace in relationships because He *is* peace. I can offer mercy and grace because He epitomizes these very qualities—they are a part of His very nature.

Recognize the significance of your relationships and the power of our own words to one another, but never make the mistake of minimizing the authority of your heavenly Father—the One who walks with you in every relationship you will ever have.

Knowing that your words have weight, and that God is the only final authority on your value and worth, write down what you know to be true about who you are as God's child.

You have a relationship with the Creator of the whole universe and He holds your future in His hands. And as you continue to embrace the principles found in this book and throughout Scripture, you get to live your life in freedom while experiencing peace—even in those "Why Can't We All Just Get Along?" relationships that will always be a part of this life.

Female Friendship at Its Best

Even though Paul didn't come on the scene until hundreds of years after they lived, I think I know a great example of two women who embodied the principles found in Romans 12. Ruth and Naomi got it right. If you are not familiar with their story, I will summarize it briefly, but you definitely want to read the whole thing in the Old Testament book of Ruth as soon as you can.

Naomi and her husband moved out of Israel during a time of intense famine. They moved to a country that did not recognize or worship their God. In that country, their two sons grew and married women from that nation. One daughter-in-law was named Orpah and the other, Ruth. Time went by and Naomi's husband passed away, soon followed by both of her sons. I cannot begin to imagine the grief in Naomi's heart. No one could have expected this. Naomi was understandably devastated.

She decided that it was time to return to her homeland and she relinquished her daughters-in-law from any obligations to her. She wanted them to know they owed her nothing and were free to remain among their own people and to marry again and have families.

Orpah agreed to accept her mother-in-law's offer of freedom. She returned to her family. But listen to the beautiful words Ruth spoke to Naomi:

> Don't urge me to leave you or to turn back from you. Where you go I will go, and where you stay I will stay. Your people will be my people and your God my God. Where you die I will die, and there I will be buried. May the LORD deal with me, be it ever so severely, if even death separates you and me (Ruth 1:16-17).

Isn't this beautiful? This is friendship at its best. Don't we all long for this kind of relationship with another woman? And Ruth was not yet a believer when she made this covenant promise to Naomi. What is even more fascinating about the friendship between Ruth and Naomi is that God chose these women to be ancestors of the One we call Savior: Jesus Christ! Wow! What an amazing story this is for all of us.

What might God want to do in our generation and those generations that come behind us through, and as a result of, our open, honest, grace-filled friendships with other women today? What might happen if each of us reading these words chose to do our part, what is up to us, to be at peace with everyone?

Let's go over this one last time...

> So here's what I want you to do, God helping you: Take your everyday, ordinary life—your sleeping, eating,

going-to-work, and walking-around life—and place it before God as an offering. Embracing what God does for you is the best thing you can do for him. Don't become so well-adjusted to your culture that you fit into it without even thinking. Instead, fix your attention on God. You will be changed from the inside out. Readily recognize what he wants from you, and quickly respond to it. Unlike the culture around you, always dragging you down to its level of immaturity, God brings the best out of you, develops well-formed maturity in you.

I'm speaking to you out of deep gratitude for all that God has given me, and especially as I have responsibilities in relation to you. Living then, as every one of you does, in pure grace, it is important that you not misinterpret yourselves as people who are bringing this goodness to God. No, God brings it all to you. The only accurate way to understand ourselves is by what God is and by what he does for us, not by what we are and what we do for him.

In this way we are like the various parts of a human body. Each part gets its meaning from the body as a whole, not the other way around. The body we're talking about is Christ's body of chosen people. Each of us finds our meaning and function as a part of his body. But as a chopped-off finger or cut-off toe we wouldn't amount to much, would we? So since we find ourselves fashioned into all these excellently formed and marvelously functioning parts in Christ's body, let's just go ahead and be what we were made to be, without enviously or pridefully comparing ourselves with each other, or trying to be something we aren't.

If you preach, just preach God's Message, nothing else; if you help, just help, don't take over; if you teach, stick to your teaching; if you give encouraging guidance, be careful that you don't get bossy; if you are put in charge, don't manipulate; if you are called to give aid to people in distress, keep your eyes open and be quick to respond; if you work

with the disadvantaged, don't let yourself get irritated with
them or depressed by them. Keep a smile on your face.
Love from the center of who you are; don't fake it. Run for
dear life from evil; hold on for dear life to good. Be good
friends who love deeply; practice playing second fiddle.

Don't burn out; keep yourselves fueled and aflame. Be
alert servants of the Master, cheerfully expectant. Don't
quit in hard times; pray all the harder. Help needy Christians; be inventive in hospitality.

Bless your enemies; no cursing under your breath.
Laugh with your happy friends when they're happy; share
tears when they're down. Get along with each other; don't
be stuck-up. Make friends with nobodies; don't be the great
somebody.

Don't hit back; discover beauty in everyone. If you've
got it in you, get along with everybody. Don't insist on getting even; that's not for you to do. "I'll do the judging," says
God. "I'll take care of it."

Our Scriptures tell us that if you see your enemy hungry, go buy that person lunch, or if he's thirsty, get him
a drink. Your generosity will surprise him with goodness.
Don't let evil get the best of you; get the best of evil by
doing good (Romans 12, MSG).

Personal Response

What prompted you to read this book in the first place? What did
you hope to gain as a result of taking this journey?

What has God shown you as you traveled this path?

What has changed in your thoughts or behaviors as a result of applying the principles found here?

Remember that person you mentioned in Chapter 1 that you would be praying for? Have your feelings changed at all when you think of this person? If so, describe the change(s).

Dear heavenly Father, what a journey this has been! Thank You for not only taking it with us, but for being our capable and encouraging Guide on each and every step. Thank You that the journey to finding lasting peace even when dealing with difficult people is just beginning! Remind us of these principles when we deal with yet another "sandpaper" person—that person who rubs us the wrong way. Help us to be aware of the times when we are this person to someone else. Make us more like You every day. In Jesus's name, amen.

Conclusion

Got Conflict?

Relationships can get sticky, but you don't have to get stuck.

To understand that relationships can be tricky and cause major problems and pain in life, all we have to do is read the story of the very first human relationships and how quickly dysfunction formed within the human race. We barely get through the first two chapters of the first book of the Bible before we begin to see the relationships falling apart. Before moving on, take a few minutes to read through Genesis 3.

The Blame Game: A Game Where Everyone Loses

Way to go, Adam! Eve didn't do much better, but at least her sin came after a conversation with the serpent. And here we see the first person ever created blame someone else for his bad decision—his sin. Do you see that? "The woman you put here with me..." (Genesis 3:12). In other words, "God, don't You see how this is really Your fault? I mean, this wouldn't have ever happened if You hadn't placed this woman here with me. I mean, I like her and all, don't get me wrong, but what were You thinking would eventually happen? She is breathtaking and delightful, so of course I'm going to do what she says. She holds all the cards here…and, um…this is Your fault. You made her this way and You gave her to me. So, You see, don't You, that this is really Your fault."

Talk about a sticky situation! Had Adam and Eve been left to themselves, they most certainly would have remained stuck—stuck blaming one another and their circumstances and stuck hiding from one another rather than relating openly and freely with each other.

It is in our nature to want to blame someone—anyone—for the problems we face. These challenges come in the form of relationship struggles, financial hardship, health issues, career woes, educational deficits…the list can go on and on. Something in us wants to hide when we're feeling threatened (as Adam and Eve did), which can look like isolation and avoidance. Or else we might go into accusing mode, attacking and blaming others—sometimes even God. The good news is that this is not news to God. He knew before He ever created Adam and Eve that all of this would go down and He already had a redemptive plan—not only in mind, but in motion. Jesus was always the Plan for mankind's redemption. Always.

You don't have to stay stuck.

This, my friend, is very good news for all of us. God knew before the foundation of the world that you and I would be a part of this world—of the human story—of God's story being written even today. And His desire to redeem your life and your history and your story is just as real today for you as it was back then for the first man and the first woman He ever created. He wanted there to be a *you* in this world. And He was willing to do whatever it took to redeem you to Himself.

I hope this reality fills you with peace and with hope. God is on His throne. He hasn't taken a leave of absence where you are concerned. And if you find yourself pulled to either isolate and avoid the conflicts you face, or attack and blame others (including your heavenly Father), I hope instead that you will pause and look heavenward to the One who knows you best, loves you most, and has a wonderful plan for your life.

I hope you will allow His Spirit to fill you while you allow His Word to nourish you.

I hope you will see Him afresh and anew. We do have an enemy, to be sure. But it isn't God.

I hope that this will help you to extend grace to those who have made life challenging for you.

Your Father Sees, Your Father Knows, and Your Father Cares

Although Adam and Eve—and you and I—missed the mark of God's perfection, God was not swayed one bit in His relationship with mankind. He still pursues us. He still sees us every single moment of every single day. He still knows us better than we know ourselves—our past, our present, and our future. And He still cares more for us than any of us can begin to fathom. This isn't a religious platitude. This is more real than anything we have ever seen with our eyes or tasted with our own tongues.

God is not an imaginary friend that we lean on for comfort or the intangible hope that we have been forgiven of our wrongdoings. He is the sovereign, all-powerful, all-knowing, ever-present Creator and Sustainer of the Universe—and He longs to be our friend. He longs for us to experience His love, His forgiveness, His grace, and yes, His delight! Let this thought envelop you as you go about your day. You are well loved by the One who created you in the secret place of your mother's womb and He pursues your heart every moment of every day.

Nothing you can do will make Him love you more and nothing you have done could make Him love you less. He loves you. He loves you. He loves *you!* And that's really something, isn't it?

Don't let this moment pass you by—jot down a prayer of response before moving on.

As I write these words the Christmas season is just getting started. I love just about everything about Christmas, but I'll tell you right up front that I do not do Black Friday. You will not get this chick anywhere near any retail shop on the day after Thanksgiving. Been there. Done that. No deal is worth the insanity! With that note aside, I love Christmas!

I love the decorations. I love the traditions. I love the holiday spirit. I love the get-togethers. I love the songs! I love the red cups at Starbucks. I just love the season. I think I love it so much because it is a season where we celebrate the good things in life. We get to remember that when the world saw its darkest hour, Light broke through in the form of a tiny baby boy.

But as much as I love Christmas, and as much as I enjoy the traditions my family celebrates, I've also dealt with some really, really painful Christmas seasons throughout my life. And, as you probably guessed by now, those painful experiences were the result of relationship troubles. Those relationships weren't always directly connected to me—some of those were relationship struggles between two other people who couldn't get along with each other. I can't tell you how many times I was screaming on the inside where no one could hear it but God and me, "It is *Christmas*, for goodness' sake! Why can't we all just get along?"

The book of Ephesians is a beautiful letter to God's people in Ephesus which still speaks loudly to God's people today. In the first three chapters, Paul teaches believers what it means to be a child of God. He describes God's incredible grace poured out to them. He describes God's immeasurable and infinite love for each one of them. He tells them what their identity was before they trusted Christ and how vastly different—brand new!—it was at the point of their salvation. And then he goes on to encourage them with a challenge to allow these truths to influence their relationships with one another:

> As a prisoner for the Lord, then, I urge you to live a life worthy of the calling you have received. Be completely humble and gentle; be patient, bearing with one another in love. Make every effort to keep the unity of the Spirit

through the bond of peace. There is one body and one Spirit, just as you were called to one hope when you were called; one Lord, one faith, one baptism; one God and Father of all, who is over all and through all and in all (Ephesians 4:1-5).

Paul knew, and taught us again and again, that community is vital for healthy growth to occur. Far too many churches and Christian organizations are preoccupied with growth, but neglect to take the time to make sure that the growth they're experiencing is healthy. Cancer grows too, y'know?

John made a similar point in one of his letters: "We love because he first loved us. Whoever claims to love God yet hates a brother or sister is a liar. For whoever does not love their brother and sister, whom they have seen, cannot love God, whom they have not seen. And he has given us this command: Anyone who loves God must also love their brother and sister" (1 John 4:19-21).

It gets pretty strict here, doesn't it? John didn't say you have to "fake it til you make it," which is an attitude many people choose over honesty. John tells us earlier that it is God's love working in us, and our trust in how loved we are, that makes us capable of this kind of generous, unconditional love. My pastor for twenty years of my life said so many times I can't count, "The Christian life is not difficult. The Christian life is impossible! This is why we need God to live it through us."

Choosing to show love to others—even those who are most difficult to love—is not impossible. In fact, God enjoys doing the impossible in our lives!

When the coworker, sister-in-law, neighbor, teacher, boss, or fellow church member is mean-spirited and underhanded, don't run away. Live out of who God says you are. Allow Him to be fully present in you and through you. You never know what impossible miracle He might be about to perform!

When you know who you are you know what to do. It's such a free place to be! I leave you with this final word of encouragement from the apostle Paul, our mentor for this entire book:

Now to him who is able to do immeasurably more than all we ask or imagine, according to his power that is at work within us, to him be glory in the church and in Christ Jesus throughout all generations, forever and ever! Amen (Ephesians 3:20-21).

Go in peace!

Leader's Guide

I can't tell you how excited I am that you have decided to participate with others in this journey to finding peace in all of our relationships! For most of my life, as a follower of Christ, I was trying to please God with the way I lived my life. The problem was that most of the time I was not measuring up. I failed. I made mistakes. I was dishonest. I felt as though the score was being kept and I was always losing points. And when other people seemed to take note of these shortcomings by the way they treated me, it seemed to only validate that false belief. If I was going to find peace—lasting and authentic peace from God and peace within my own heart—I was going to have to listen to His voice speaking through His Word. And I was going to have to decide whether or not I would believe and then follow what it said.

As you lead or facilitate your small group discussions and study, you will encounter other women with these same kinds of struggles—and perhaps you are one of them. Keep this in mind as you share conversations and questions. May grace and safety rule over any perceived need to put doctrine or preference above someone's heart.

As you lead a small group through the discussion questions listed here, along with the questions and comments found throughout the chapters, then please hear my heart: Even as I write these words, I am sincerely praying for you as a leader or facilitator of the materials found here. It is my greatest hope and expectation that our heavenly Father will equip you with wisdom as you follow His guidance.

Because relationships can be so challenging at times, remember the grace policy we'll use in our small group discussions: It is always better to err on the side of grace. Deal? This means that it is more important that we listen to one another and that each person feels heard than it is that any of us be "right."

If you have questions or comments as you go through this book and the discussion questions together, please feel free to email us at info@ church4chicks.com. I can't promise that we can get back to every question right away, but we will be intentional to read and respond to all that we can.

Ready? Let's do this!

Optional ideas to help your small group time be more effective:

1. Alternate who leads the facilitation of the discussion each time you meet. This gives everyone an opportunity to use their gifts to enhance the group's time together.

2. Set boundaries for your time together before you have the first meeting. This will help you all stay focused, on track, and keep anyone from feeling pressured to stay beyond what is comfortable. She'll know up front what the expectations are for the meeting times.

3. Let your very first meeting be a social time. This will help everyone break the ice and enjoy getting to know each other in a casual setting before diving into the deep stuff with (possibly) new people.

4. Make sure everyone has a chance to respond, but don't mandate that everyone do so. Sometimes we need a little bit of space and grace for genuine, Spirit-led growth to occur.

5. Utilize the questions contained within the chapters that you believe will be conducive to your small group's discussions.

6. It is not as important that every question be discussed as it is that everyone gets to share in the discussion. The goal is to find peace in our own lives even in the midst of difficult relationships. These questions are meant to help engage participants in discussion, so don't sweat it too much if some of the questions don't make it to the table.

7. I want to caution you as you lead to be careful to not become the "teacher" of the group. Facilitating discussion, helping the group stay on topic as much as possible, and ensuring that everyone has a chance to speak will go a lot further than turning the small group time into another lecture from one voice alone.

8. Pray, pray, pray for one another often! Actually, this one isn't optional. It is an absolute necessity. Prayer fuels the freedom to have open discussion, experience spiritual growth, and find protection for the assault of the enemy. He is not going to just sit and watch your relationships get better—he's going to oppose. But don't fret: God is bigger, better, and smarter. And besides, Proverbs 21:30 makes us a great promise: "There is no wisdom, no insight, no plan that can succeed against the Lord." Keep this promise in mind (and perhaps written down somewhere to remind you and your group often) as you take this journey together.

Chapter 1: It's Not You. It's Me.

We need a God-centered approach to life.

1. Why do you believe God desires to be the center of your life?

2. How is God's glory best made known through relationships?

3. What was your most influential friendship in childhood? Teen years? How did these relationships (or this one relationship) help shape you into the person you are today?

4. It has been said that our friends determine the direction of our life. How can you see this reality in your own life?

5. How did your relationship with God begin? Who was it that most influenced you into His direction?

Chapter 2: What's Love Got to Do with It?

Loved people love people. It is vital that we embrace the truth that we are dearly and well loved by God.

1. In this chapter, Julie shares that trust is often the factor missing in relationships—especially among women. Many women struggle to have close friendships with other women. Discuss this reality and any personal stories that members of the group would like to share.

2. John 13:35 says, "By this everyone will know that you are my disciples, if you love one another." Why do you think God would make this the true test of His followers?

3. Women have a biological, built-in need for friendship with other women. How do you see this reality in your own life and in the lives of women you know?

4. Sometimes it is easier to see and believe God's love for others more readily than we can embrace this truth for ourselves. Take a few minutes and affirm God's love for the others within the group. (An example might be: "Sharon, I can definitely see God's love for you when I look at the path He has you on in this season of your life. Although your journey hasn't been an easy one, I am filled with hope for you because I know He loves you so much." Or, "Daisy,

I can totally recognize God's love for you! Your energy and enthusiasm for life are a reflection of His very nature in you.")

Chapter 3: Created for Relationship

God designed our relationships with the purpose of revealing His glory.

1. Our greatest wounds come through relationship, but so does our greatest healing. Discuss this idea and how you've found yourself on both sides of this reality.

2. What (if any) challenges have you faced in recent days, even this week or today, that have created a wound as it pertains to your relationships? How did you handle that challenge?

3. Share with your small group your most vivid memory from junior high. How did this experience from your adolescent years impact you the most?

4. Describe a healthy relationship that you have observed. What characteristics of that relationship make it so strong?

5. What is your desire for your own relationships going forward? Is there one in particular that your small group/partner can pray with you about?

Chapter 4: The Pressure Is Off!

The only true path to freedom (which yields lasting peace) is the one that finds us living as sacrifices to our God.

1. Discuss together what it means to be a living sacrifice.

2. Why do you believe this is the place of our greatest freedom?

3. We have all wished, at one time or another, that we had a direct line to God to find out what we should do in a given

situation. Read Romans 12:1-2 together. What does this passage say about this topic?

4. There is a big difference between conforming and transforming. Discuss these differences together and share example of what each can look like in your lives.

5. Read Romans 12:3 together. If "humility is having a proper estimation of yourself based on what God says of you," then it is important for us to know what God says about us, right? Discuss the truths you know about what God says about His children. You may want to share some biblical passages with one another.

Chapter 5: Know Thyself

Humility attracts grace.

1. The most honestly humble people you'll meet are the ones who have the healthiest concept of who they are. How was the trait of humility modeled to you as a child? How is humility most often displayed in the Church?

2. Why do you believe that it is our humility that attracts God's grace?

3. Why is it that pride repels His grace?

4. Why do you believe it's so hard for us to get this balance of humility and maintain it?

5. Seeing yourself as God sees you is how humility plays itself out in your life. What does the Bible have to say about who we are and what is most true about us?

Chapter 6: Big Girls *Do* Cry

Women who tend to become critics, cynics, and competitors do so out of their own insecurities, which are the inevitable results of identity confusion.

1. In Chapter 6, we learn of a pastor who stated that the most painful experiences of his life were not in losing his four-year-old son in a freak accident while on vacation, but in witnessing wounds inflicted between Christian brothers and sisters. Can you identify at all with this pastor's statement? If so, how?

2. Have you ever met a cynic, critic, or competitor? Which one of these characteristics is your bent? What did you learn about yourself as you read this section?

3. Competition can be healthy when its purpose is to bring out the best in both parties. Discuss when you've seen this result of healthy competition.

4. Discuss ways that you can pray for, encourage, and hold one another accountable (in a grace-filled way—no score-keeping here!) this week.

Chapter 7: Pom-Poms Are One-Size-Fits-All

There is hope for all of us! Regardless of the dysfunctional ways we relate to others, God can transform us into women who make this world a better place!

1. Do you remember the old show or movie based on the play entitled "The Odd Couple" about two roommates who were complete opposites? Felix and Oscar were night and day different in the way they handled conflict, housekeeping, and everything else. It made for great comedy to watch, but it isn't all that funny in real life to live out. Discuss why opposites don't always attract.

2. Why do you suppose our heavenly Father intentionally puts us in these "Odd Couple" relationships?

3. In this chapter, we look at the basic differences between extroverts and introverts. Why do you think we feel the pull so often to make other people become more like us and struggle so much with people who are different from us?

4. Describe someone you know who reflects the qualities of a cheerleader to others.

5. Be a cheerleader to one another. Take some time to encourage the hearts of those within your small group. Get creative in how you do this. Have fun!

Chapter 8: We Are Family!

We have all received Motivational Gifts of the Spirit and God intends for us to use them to build up the Body of Christ, blessing one another and the world in which we live.

1. The Seven Motivational Gifts of the Holy Spirit are shared briefly in this chapter. Take some time together, either as a whole group or in smaller groups, to talk about these gifts. Do you know what your gifts are? How did you discover them? How are you developing them? How are you dispensing them?

2. Read Ephesians 4:7-16 together and discuss the following:

    a. In verse 7, what word does the apostle Paul use to describe the gifts Christ gives us?

    b. In verses 12-13, Paul gives us a pretty significant reason these gifts exist. What is this reason?

    c. Verse 14 describes that this kind of understanding, as we mature in Christ, offers us protection. How so?

    d. Living things grow. They either grow in health or they

grow in disease. Read verses 15-16 and discuss what healthy growth in a believer looks like.

3. Consider what life could look like in your home, community, church, and workplace if believers would use their gifts to build up those around them. Discuss how you, as members of your group, can take steps toward using your own gifts in the lives of others.

Chapter 9: Live *Your* Life

Live the life God has given *you*. Live out of the reality of your true identity—not what anyone else has said, but what God declares to be true.

1. Why is it so important for believers to have clarity on their identity in Christ?

2. How is your identity as a believer different now than it was before you came to know Christ?

3. What was your first impression of God?

4. How has your concept of God changed (if at all) since that first impression?

5. Quoted in this chapter is the comment, "We respect strength, but we connect at weakness." Discuss this comment and its meaning. Do you agree or disagree, and why?

Chapter 10: I Get By with a Little Help from My Friends

Choose your friends very carefully because your friends determine the direction your life is heading.

1. We all have a God-given need to find security and significance, and it's God's intention that we find Him as a Source. Oftentimes, though, we will look to alternate

sources rather than to our Creator. How have you seen this play out in your life?

2. Read Jeremiah 2:13. We are all guilty of digging our own cisterns—our own sources—for life. Discuss a time in your life when you were digging your own cisterns. How will you combat this temptation in the future?

3. Which girl are you? Are you the one who tries hard to make friends or the one who is sought out by others for friendship? Why?

4. Why do you suppose women have so many more challenges in friendships than guys do?

5. The Bible teaches us that we need to be cautious in friendship and choose our friends wisely. What attributes do you believe make for a really good friend?

Chapter 11: Off the Hook

We've heard it before. We'll hear it again. We must forgive!

1. Why do you think we tend to view other women as a threat? Where do you think this comes from?

2. How should we combat the temptation to form an unhealthy alliance ("negative bonding") with another woman when we sense a threat?

3. In Matthew 18, Jesus teaches us that forgiveness boils down to the releasing of a debt owed. Why do you think this is such an important topic with our Lord?

4. "Forgiveness and trust are not twins." How would you explain this to someone else?

5. "God will not ever take from one of His children to give to another." How does this principle bring comfort to your life/situation/past experiences?

Chapter 12: Conflict and Confrontation

As we grow in wisdom, we become better equipped to know when and how to handle conflict and confrontation.

1. Why do you suppose conflict and confrontation are so challenging for most females?

2. How have you seen other women handle disputes? Give both positive and negative examples (without sharing names).

3. This chapter contains questions to consider before confronting someone. Discuss with one another how asking these questions before choosing to confront someone can help you handle an uncomfortable situation.

4. Discuss with one another your personal bent to handling conflict: Do you avoid the other person or do you push for engagement? How can you find balance as you move forward?

Chapter 13: Grace Under Fire

We represent Jesus best when we offer grace to others. (Remember, if it can be earned, it ceases to be grace.)

1. Have you been taught to find revenge by killing others with kindness? Describe a time when you did this.

2. What is your response to God's perspective on "heaping burning coals of fire on their heads"?

3. How would you define, describe, and explain God's grace to someone who has little or no experience with it?

4. What are some practical ways we can show grace to those around us?

5. Read 2 Peter 1:3 together. What do you have specifically and how does this help you to live a godly life?

6. God is the only One who can be angry and still make the right choice in that anger. How does this idea comfort you when you think of your own life and the lives of those you love?

Chapter 14: A Future Worth Looking Forward To

When we choose to live by God's principles found in Scripture, we give ourselves a future worth looking forward to.

1. When you were a kid, what did you want to be when you grew up? Did that wish become a reality?

2. We all have regrets. We all have items on our life's résumé that we wish we could remove. How can you see the grace of God in your life even with those items and regrets in place?

3. How do you think you can adopt a mindset that gives you a "future worth looking forward to"?

4. How can we allow God to use us to help others with this as well?

Thank you for taking this journey, not only with me, but with one another! This is one of those realities in life that doesn't go away just because we have success once or twice. It is an ongoing battle. The enemy is after your peace, my friend, and he will not play fair and he certainly will not fight fair.

The good news is that we can be well equipped with God's armor for those battles when they come. The better news is that there don't have to be any casualties of war!

Church 4 Chicks

Helping women live with purpose…without the pressure!

Ask women what they feel today and you'll hear a variety of answers. If they feel comfortable enough to say it like it *really* is, most of those answers will reveal that underneath it all, we feel pressure.

We feel guilty for being too much of one thing and not enough of another. We feel guarded around others because life experience tells us we can't really trust. We've felt the sting of rejection when we don't measure up to someone else's expectations or standards. We feel pulled in all kinds of directions.

At C4C, we offer women a safe place that is *free* from all of those pressures. Church 4 Chicks will help you:

- escape the pressure of trying to measure up to unrealistic standards
- enjoy deeper, unguarded relationships with women of all ages
- live fully in your own skin as you embrace your incredible value and worth
- drop the shackles of past wounds and false beliefs that have kept you from your unique destiny
- pass along this contagious freedom to others

At C4C, it is our passion to create and cultivate these kinds of environments of grace for women of all ages. C4C is a come-as-you-are environment where you are free to be you. A place where you can breathe deeply and connect unreservedly with others. We invite you to experience this for yourself at one of our live events. For more info, visit our events page and connect on our website. We look forward to seeing you soon!

The purpose of Church 4 Chicks is to be used of God to create an environment of authenticity, a balance of grace and truth, and dynamic worship through music and teaching where women of all ages, denominational affiliations, and backgrounds can come together to experience an authentic encounter with God, while cultivating deeper relationships with others.

For more information and to connect with us online, please visit us at
www.church4chicks.com
and on Facebook and Twitter!

About the Author

Shelley Hendrix helps women live with purpose...*without* the pressure! She is a wife, mother, Bible teacher, speaker, author, and television talk show host—but more important than any role she fills, she is most grateful to be a child of God, learning to live out of who God says she is. Shelley has been referred to as the "strongest female communicator on the topic of grace in our generation." Shelley has been teaching at her home church and various venues since 1997. She is a host of "Atlanta Live!"—a Christian talk show on Atlanta's WATC TV 57. Shelley speaks at various events nationwide. Shelley is honored to be married to her best friend, Stephen. They have three amazing children (whom God uses to teach them much!) and live in Atlanta, Georgia.

Find out more about Shelley and how to connect with her
for your next event at
www.church4chicks.com or at www.shelleyhendrix.com

Notes

1. Shelley E. Taylor et al. "Behavioral Responses to Stress: Tend and Befriend, Not Fight or Flight." *Psychological Review* 107, no. 3 (2000): 411-429.

2. Rick Renner, *Sparkling Gems from the Greek: 365 Greek Word Studies for Every Day of the Year to Sharpen Your Understanding of God's Word* (Tulsa, OK: Teach All Nations, 2003), 77.

3. For this sentiment, and much else, I am indebted to Pastor Andy Stanley of North Point Community Church in Alpharetta, Georgia.

4. I learned this phrase from the TrueFaced Message by John Lynch, Bruce McNicol, and Bill Thrall. I highly recommend their resources! www.truefaced.com.

5. A.W. Tozer, *The Knowledge of the Holy* (San Francisco: Harper and Row Publishers, 1961), 1.

6. Joel Hunter, Twitter post, June 9, 2010, 8:19 a.m., http://twitter.com/northlandchurch.

7. Cindy Beall, *Healing Your Marriage When Trust Is Broken* (Eugene, OR: Harvest House Publishers, 2011), 45.

8. Corrie ten Boom, *The Hiding Place* (Ada, MI: Chosen Books, 2006), 248.

To learn more about Harvest House books and
to read sample chapters, log on to our website:

www.harvesthousepublishers.com

HARVEST HOUSE PUBLISHERS
EUGENE, OREGON